W9-BAL-801

CULTURE SMART!
MALAYSIA

Victor T. King

·K·U·P·E·R·A·R·D·

This book is available for special discounts for bulk purchases for sales promotions or premiums. Special editions, including personalized covers, excerpts of existing books, and corporate imprints, can be created in large quantities for special needs.

For more information in the USA write to Special Markets/Premium Sales, 1745 Broadway, MD 6–2, New York, NY 10019, or e-mail specialmarkets@randomhouse.com.

In the United Kingdom contact Kuperard publishers at the address below.

ISBN 978 1 85733 457 9
This book is also available as an e-book: eISBN 978 1 85733 611 5

British Library Cataloguing in Publication Data
A CIP catalogue entry for this book is available from the British Library

First published in Great Britain
by Kuperard, an imprint of Bravo Ltd
59 Hutton Grove, London N12 8DS
Tel: +44 (0) 20 8446 2440   Fax: +44 (0) 20 8446 2441
www.culturesmart.co.uk
Inquiries: sales@kuperard.co.uk

Distributed in the United States and Canada
by Random House Distribution Services
1745 Broadway, New York, NY 10019
Tel: +1 (212) 572-2844   Fax: +1 (212) 572-4961
Inquiries: csorders@randomhouse.com

Series Editor Geoffrey Chesler
Design Bobby Birchall

Printed in Malaysia

Cover image: The Petronas Towers, Kuala Lumpur. *Travel Ink/Geoffrey Clive*
Images on pages 15, 16, 17, 30, 77, 81, 92, 98, 105, 106, 115, 119, and 123 courtesy of Tourism Malaysia

Images on pages 34 and 61 © www.othermalaysia.org; 38 © Brian Jeffery Beggerly; 39 © Cayce; 40 © amrufm; 41 and 121 © Gryffindor; 55 © bbbsheep; 58 © www.pachd.com; 109 © Terence Ong; 116 © Goh Wei Zhong; 125 © Henryk Kotoviski

About the Author

VICTOR KING is Professor of South-East Asian Studies at the University of Leeds and Executive Director of the White Rose East Asia Center, a joint research–training venture in Chinese and Japanese Studies between the East Asian Studies departments at Leeds and Sheffield. He spent most of his career in the University of Hull, where he was Director of the Center for South-East Asian Studies, Dean of Social and Political Sciences, Director of the Graduate School, and Pro-Vice-Chancellor. He has undertaken anthropological and sociological research on Indonesia, Malaysia, and Brunei, and supervised research projects on these and other countries. A frequent visitor to Malaysia and the wider region, he has written extensively on its societies and cultures. He has recently coauthored an anthropological study of Southeast Asia, written an introduction to the sociology of change in the region, and coedited a book on tourism in Southeast Asia.

**The Culture Smart! series is continuing to expand.
For further information and latest titles visit
www.culturesmart.co.uk**

The publishers would like to thank **CultureSmart!**Consulting for its help in researching and developing the concept for this series.

CultureSmart!Consulting creates tailor-made seminars and consultancy programs to meet a wide range of corporate, public-sector, and individual needs. Whether delivering courses on multicultural team building in the USA, preparing Chinese engineers for a posting in Europe, training call-center staff in India, or raising the awareness of police forces to the needs of diverse ethnic communities, it provides essential, practical, and powerful skills worldwide to an increasingly international workforce.

For details, visit www.culturesmartconsulting.com

CultureSmart!Consulting and **CultureSmart!** guides have both contributed to and featured regularly in the weekly travel program "Fast Track" on BBC World TV.

contents

contents

Map of Malaysia

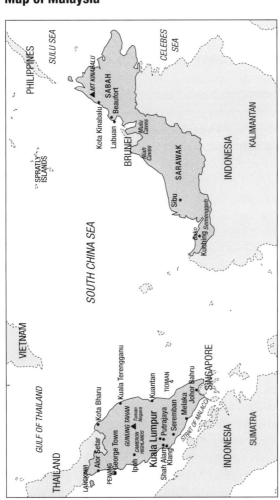

introduction

The Federation of Malaysia, a nation of 27 million people and a constitutional monarchy and democracy, is one of the successful newly industrializing countries of the Asia Pacific region. Formerly a relatively small but economically vital part of the British Empire, and a major exporter of the primary products of tin and rubber, Malaysia now has a diversified economic profile. It is still an important source of natural resources and tropical agricultural products—petroleum, natural gas, tin, copper, iron ore, bauxite, sawn timber and wood products, rattan, palm oil, pepper, coconut, pineapple, and rubber—but it is also a manufacturer of electrical and electronic goods, textiles, vehicles, and chemicals, with a growing services sector including a fast expanding tourism industry. It pursues a relatively open-door economic policy and plays an active role in regional and other international organizations.

In many respects Malaysia is a modern nation-state, and from a predominantly rural society in the immediate postwar years it has become an increasingly urbanized one. Nevertheless, elements of the traditional past remain. The country still presents the visitor with an exciting and fascinating medley of cultures—Malay, Chinese, Indian, Arab, Eurasian, Dayak, and aboriginal. These communities have retained, though in a much changed form, a considerable amount of their cultural heritage, and Malaysia continues to demonstrate the virtues of a culturally diverse, exotic, and vibrant "plural society" in customs, religion, festivals, costume, cuisine, language, and architecture.

To help foreign visitors and residents navigate this rich and complex cultural mix, *Culture Smart! Malaysia* provides a succinct and straightforward introduction to Malaysian history and society. It explains the deeper core values of the different ethnic groups, and guides you through Malaysian etiquette and behavior so that you might be inclined to do the right rather than the wrong things. "Human intelligence" is key to successful relationships. But nothing is guaranteed in a globalized world. We all take our chances and hope that we are sufficiently sensitive to be able to survive those awkward cross-cultural moments.

This is a guide, not a definitive document on what should or should not be done in a variety of situations. Much of what is provided here is based on common sense, and assumes that when we encounter people of other cultures we all try to behave reasonably. It can tell you what might offend and what might please, but ultimately it's up to the reader to respond positively to another culture, to engage, relate, interact, and understand. If you have a passion for learning about other cultures, then stay with us on this journey to Malaysia!

Key Facts

Official Name	The Federation of Malaysia (Persekutuan Tanah Malaysia)	
Capital City	Kuala Lumpur	Pop. 1.58 million (2006 estimate); 6.9 million (metropolitan area)
Administrative Capital	Putrajaya	There are 13 states: 11 on the Malay Peninsula and 2 on the island of Borneo.
Federal States and Territories	States: Johor, Kedah, Kelantan, Melaka, Negeri Sembilan, Pahang, Perak, Perlis, Pulau Pinang, Sabah, Sarawak, Selangor, and Terengganu. Federal territory: cities of Kuala Lumpur, Labuan, and Putrajaya	
Major Towns and Cities	Penang (George Town) (Pulau Pinang), Ipoh, Klang, Malacca (Melaka), Johor Bahru, Kuching, Sibu, Kota Kinabalu, Alor Setar, Shah Alam, Kota Bharu, Kuantan, Kuala Terengganu, Seremban	
Population	27.1 million (2007 est.)	Growth rate, 1.8% per annum; birthrate 22.7 per thousand; life expectancy, 72.8 years
Area	127,355 sq. miles (329, 848 sq. km)	
Climate	Tropical, hot and humid, more moderate in highlands	Sea level temperature range 77–91.5 °F (25–33 °C) throughout the year
Currency	Malaysian ringgit (RM or dollar)	Approx. $ M6.9 = £1 sterling; $ M3.49= US $1
GDP	US $313.8 billion (2006)	Economic growth rate 5.2% (2005 est.)

Ethnic Make-up	Malays (50.4%); Chinese (23.7%); Indians (7.1%); other indigenous (11%) including Dayaks (Ibans, Bidayuhs, Melanaus, Kayans, Kenyahs, Kadazan-Dusuns, Muruts), and *Orang Asli*; others (7.8%) incl. Eurasians, Arabs, and non-Malaysians	
Language	Bahasa Malaysia/Malay (or Bahasa Melayu), Mandarin and Chinese dialects (Cantonese, Hokkien, Hakka, Hainanese, Foochow), Tamil, Punjabi, Telugu, Malayalam; English is widely spoken.	
Adult Literacy	88.7% (2004)	
Religions	Muslim, Christian (Protestant, Catholic), Buddhist, Hindu, Sikh	
Government	Federal constitutional monarchy. The king, selected on a five-year rotation, appoints the prime minister from the largest party in the elected lower house.	Elected House of Representatives (*Dewan Rakyat*) and nonelected Senate (*Dewan Negara*). Nine states have hereditary sultans and four states appointed governors.
Media	TV and radio channels in Bahasa Malaysia and English	Newspapers and magazines in Bahasa Malaysia, English, Mandarin, Chinese dialects, Tamil, and Hindi
Electricity	240 volts, 50 Hz	3-prong plugs, compatible with UK
TV/Video	PAL system, compatible with UK	
Internet Domain	.my	
Telephone	Malaysia's country code is 60.	The code for Kuala Lumpur is (0)3.
Time Zone	GMT + 8 hours	

LAND &
PEOPLE

GEOGRAPHICAL SNAPSHOT

Malaysia extends over 127,355 square miles (329,848 sq. km) of territory, with significantly over half its land area in the two northern Borneo states of Sarawak and Sabah (formerly British North Borneo). The Malaysian Borneo states are 620 miles (approximately1,000 km) long and 155 miles (250 km) at their widest point. The most prominent feature of Malaysia's geography is the division between peninsular Malaysia (sometimes, contentiously, referred to as "West Malaysia")—where the capital city, Kuala Lumpur, and the newly created administrative capital of Putrajaya are located—and Malaysian Borneo (equally contentiously referred to as "East Malaysia"), the two major parts of the country being separated by a wide expanse of the South China Sea, at the closest point some 398 miles (640 km) across. Much of Malaysia is relatively thinly populated, particularly the great state of Sarawak, and overall population density is around 32 per square mile (about 82 per sq. km), though most Malaysians live on the western side of the peninsula from Pulau Pinang (Penang) in the north through Kuala

Lumpur and Klang and on to Johor Bahru in the south, situated at the causeway that joins Malaysia to the Republic of Singapore. Malaysia's colonial legacy and the British focus on tin mining and rubber cultivation help to explain the uneven or unbalanced character of the population and the economy. The most densely populated, economically advanced, and cosmopolitan parts of the country are to be found precisely in those areas where tin and rubber were exploited and where the British developed an administrative, commercial, and communications infrastructure.

CLIMATE

Malaysia, located in the humid Asian tropics between latitudes 1 and 7°, has a monsoonal, equatorial climate. It is hot, humid, and wet; those from cooler and temperate climes might describe it as "very hot, very humid, and very wet." For the first-time visitor the sensation is of having one's face and head covered with a hot, wet towel. Some geographers distinguish seasonal differences in

that the monsoon wind pattern provides some variation in rainfall, but not much in temperature. Temperatures are uniformly high, usually ranging between 77 and 91.5°F (between about 25 and 33°C) at sea level, but some nights can be considerably cooler, and most nights are comfortably warm at about 70–71°F (21–22°C). The British colonials often retreated to the hill stations, where temperatures in the Cameron and Genting Highlands in peninsular Malaysia are a few degrees lower.

After heavy rainfall the heat also subsides somewhat, but prior to rain the heat and humidity can be quite overpowering, and as high as 90 percent; the average year-round humidity is about 80 percent. After heavy rain there is a freshness in the atmosphere and pleasant smells that come from the intermingling of water and vegetation. Malaysia experiences two major monsoonal cycles: the southwest monsoon prevails roughly from May to September/October, and the northeast monsoon from October/November to March/April. The start and end of the monsoon seasons is variable. The northeast monsoon in particular brings heavy rain to the coasts of Malaysian Borneo and the east coast of the peninsula; in these areas annual rainfall levels can reach up to 200 inches (5,080 mm). Average annual rainfall ranges from 80 to 100 inches (roughly 2,000 to 2,500 mm), and the number of rainy days per year in Kuala Lumpur is normally around 200. There is also little seasonal variation in the length of day and night, with the sun rising around 6:00 a.m. and setting around 6:00 p.m.

LANDSCAPE

Another significant element of the environment is that every state has a coastline; its length is about 2,905 miles (4,675 km) in total. A considerable area of Malaysia also comprises relatively rugged upland terrain rising to a height of 13,435 feet (4,095 m) with Mount Kinabalu in Sabah, the highest mountain in Southeast Asia, now a majestic national park. Parts of the main range in peninsular Malaysia reach 5,580 feet (1,700 m); one of the highest points is 7,185 feet (2,190 m) at Gunung Tahan in the Titiwangsa range. Most of the country is over 985 feet (300 m) above sea level, but there are also extensive areas of lowland mangrove and peat swamp, particularly along the western parts of peninsular Malaysia and in long stretches of coastal Sarawak and eastern Sabah. Some of the best beaches are located on the east coast of the peninsula, and on islands like

Langkawi, Penang, and Tioman with their developed resorts; the islands conjure up all the established images of the tropical paradise, with

warm, golden sands, clear blue seas, coral reefs, and palm-fringed beaches, where the colors are startlingly bright and clear.

Even up until about thirty years ago much of the country, particularly the uplands, would have been covered by dense tropical rain forests, but commercial logging, farming, road building, and residential development have taken their toll. Large areas of the country, especially in the rolling foothills, have also been developed for plantation agriculture, particularly oil palm, natural rubber, tea, and cocoa. However, the Malaysian government, recognizing the deleterious effects of human-induced environmental change, has developed a relatively vigorous approach to the establishment of national parks, forest reserves, and wildlife sanctuaries. The number of these is quite staggering: more than twenty national parks, mainly in Sarawak; more than thirty wildlife and nature reserves and sanctuaries, with more than twenty in peninsular Malaysia, and a hundred-plus forest reserves, many of them in Sabah. Pristine rain forests, palms, lianas,

Rafflesia, pitcher plants, orchids, towering uplands, rapids, waterfalls, limestone caves and pinnacles, orangutans, gibbons, macaques, proboscis monkeys, monitor lizards, deer,

wild boar, and birds of paradise beckon the
overseas visitor in search of something different.

THE PEOPLE

The total population of Malaysia is estimated
(June 2007) at just over 27 million, more than
80 percent of them living in the peninsula.

The politically dominant
Muslim Malays make up
roughly half of the
population (about
13.5 million). The
Chinese constitute just
under a quarter (roughly
6.5 million), and the
Indians just over 7 percent (just under 2 million).
The remainder of the indigenous population,
comprising the *orang asli*, or aborigines of the
peninsula, and the Dayaks of Borneo, make up a
further 11 percent (about 3 million). The "other"
populations include Eurasians, Arabs, and non-
Malaysian communities from other parts of Asia
and beyond (about 7 percent).

   In the Malaysian Constitution the Malays and
the Dayaks are categorized as "indigenes," or
bumiputera (literally, "sons of the soil"). Unlike
the Malays, the Dayaks, who were famed as head-
hunters and longhouse dwellers, are primarily
non-Muslim; they are also divided into a large
number of what are popularly called "tribes," or
ethnic groupings. However, the Dayaks comprise

more than half the population of Sarawak and
about two-thirds of the population of Sabah. One
of the major Dayak communities is the Ibans of
Sarawak, who number about 600,000. The *orang
asli* have a separate constitutional status as
"aboriginals," and though for certain purposes
they are seen as indigenous, like the Malays and
the natives of Sarawak and Sabah, they do not
have the same special privileges.

It is important to note that Malaysia's dramatic
economic growth during the past thirty years has
resulted in a rapidly increasing need for labor that
cannot be satisfied in the domestic market. There
may be more than 2 million migrant workers in
Malaysia, mainly from Indonesia, Thailand, the
Philippines, and the Indian subcontinent. They
are heavily involved in the plantation,
construction, and services sectors, and significant
numbers reside in the country illegally.

This is a very simplified picture of a much more
ethnically complex reality. The three broad ethnic
categories of Malays, Chinese, and Indians are
internally differentiated so that Muslim Malays
comprise a mix of people, some long-established on
the peninsula, but many of them descended from
relatively recent migrants from the Indonesian
islands to the south. The Chinese are made up of a
relatively diverse range of communities tracing their
descent mainly from southern China, including
Hokkien, Hakka, Cantonese, Teochiu, Hainanese,
and Foochow. Indians are differentiated internally
by religion (primarily Hindus, Sikhs, and Muslims),

caste, homeland, or origin in India, occupation, and language. In Malaysia there are Tamils, Bengalis, Gujeratis, Chulias, Parsees, and Malayalis, to name only the most prominent groups. There are also interesting hybrid communities derived from intermarriage and cultural exchange: there are Eurasians derived usually from relations between European men and local women during the colonial period; then the Baba, Peranakan, or Straits Chinese, long-settled in the former Straits Settlements, who combine elements of Chinese and Malay culture, including a delicious hybrid cuisine; the Jawi Peranakan, or Muslim Indians of mixed Indian and Malay descent; and the Indian Babas or Melaka Chittys who are of Hindu Indian descent but who have absorbed much of the local Malay culture.

These multiple divisions were gradually rationalized and simplified in censuses and in constitutional and administrative terms during the British colonial period and in the postwar years. Political party formation also contributed to this process as broad ethnic categories—Malays, Chinese, and Indians, as well as Dayaks—became associated with particular political parties and their supporting associations. The indigenous population, especially the Malays, enjoy certain constitutional privileges in such areas as employment, business, higher education, and political life; these were strengthened formally in the context of the New Economic Policy launched in 1970. The main areas of politics, and particularly the key ministries (Finance, Defense, Foreign

Affairs, and Education) and decision making are the preserve of the Malays.

A BRIEF HISTORY
Trade and Religion

The lands that now comprise the Federation of Malaysia straddle the great sea routes between India and China and provided a meeting point for merchants, sailors, travelers, and pilgrims carried by the monsoonal winds across the Indian Ocean, the Bay of Bengal, and the South China Sea. They also served as commercial and exchange points for traders carrying local goods within the Malay-Indonesian archipelago. For this reason Malaysia, particularly the peninsula and the coastline bordering the strategically important Straits of Malacca (Melaka), has long been a focus for maritime trade. Early in the first millennium CE the coasts of what was popularly called the Malayan or Malay Peninsula, and known by the Indians originally as the "Golden Chersonese," were the location of small trading states, visited by Indian, Chinese, and Middle Eastern merchants and traders. These early kingdoms embraced variants of Indian Hinduism and Buddhism and Indian court culture and statecraft, and for a time came under the control of larger states like Buddhist Srivijaya, further south in Sumatra and Java in what is now

Indonesia. Indeed, the lands in the two neighboring countries of what came to be called Malaysia and Indonesia, along with Singapore and Brunei, were seen as interconnected and a part of seaborne states that based their power on control of strategic ports, harbors, and seaways. Subsequently the great religion of trade, Islam, began to be established along the coasts of Sumatra, Java, and the Malayan Peninsula during the eleventh and twelfth centuries. Sunni Islam and such traditions as Sufism were brought to Southeast Asia via India by Arab, Persian, and north Indian teachers, holy men, and traders, and the local rulers and elites whose states were involved in Asian trade began to be converted to this new and powerful religion. Conversion was not the result of military intervention and subjugation; it was instead a relatively peaceful process of social, economic, and cultural interaction, cultural exchange, and intermarriage. Local Malay and other rulers recognized the importance as well as the political and economic advantages of embracing this rapidly expanding and internationalized religion.

Malacca

One such Muslim Malay state and entrepot, which rose to prominence in the fifteenth century, was Malacca (now transcribed as Melaka), occupying a strategic position overlooking the Straits and involved in the long-distance trade of valuable spices (including pepper, cloves, mace, and nutmeg), precious metals, tin, textiles, porcelain, silks, and exotic tropical produce such as camphor and aromatic sandalwood. Malaysian history did not begin with Malacca, but until recently the government, preoccupied with raising the importance of Malay culture and achievements in national history, declared that Malacca was "where it all began" in the early fifteenth century. Malay culture and language developed in southern Sumatra (and also western Borneo) and the archaeological and historical evidence suggests that the Buddhist trading kingdom of Srivijaya, which emerged in the seventh century CE in the area of what is now Palembang, was an early Malay political center. However, it was the commercial and political success of Malacca that led to the dissemination of Islam and Malay culture through the Malay-Indonesian archipelago and into the southern Philippines.

Oral traditions say that Malacca was founded by a Hindu-Buddhist prince, possibly of Srivijayan origin, Parameswara, but one of his immediate successors converted to Islam probably during the early fifteenth century. Malacca became very prosperous under Sultans Muzaffar Shah and Mansur. Mansur was also ably supported by his distinguished lieutenants, Tun Perak, Tun Ali, and Hang Tuah, who occupy a special place in Malay historical annals and whose characters, values, and wisdom have served as role models for subsequent Malay leaders and heroes.

The Portuguese

Had it not been for the increasing intervention of the ambitious Iberian states of Portugal and Spain in maritime Southeast Asia from the sixteenth century, it is most probable that the conversion of Hindu-Buddhist and pagan communities to Islam would have continued apace, or have accelerated. Malay sultanates were subsequently established throughout the Malayan Peninsula, and in northwest Borneo; the territories that later became known as Sarawak and Sabah were subject to the Brunei sultanate, and parts of Sabah later came under competing Muslim polities in the Sulu and Mindanao region of the southern Philippines. The Portuguese reported that the Brunei ruler did not convert to Islam until the early sixteenth century but Brunei managed to maintain suzerainty over most of the surrounding northern coasts of Borneo until the increasing intervention of British traders and adventurers from the mid-nineteenth century.

It is no surprise that the Portuguese as the preeminent European trading nation in Asia in the sixteenth century decided that Malacca, as the focal point of the spice trade, and as a center of Muslim-Malay power, must be defeated. Portugal and Spain were attracted to the region by the riches that control of the spice trade brought, by their desire to counter the power and influence of Islam and Muslim trade through Southeast Asia,

India, the Middle East, and the Mediterranean, and to secure recruits for Christianity. The first Portuguese expedition east of India arrived at Malacca in 1509. Two years later under Afonso de Albuquerque they captured Malacca from Sultans Mahmud Shah and Ahmad Shah. Malacca became the center of the Portuguese seaborne empire in the east. However, very little of the Portuguese legacy in Malacca remains, other than the stone gateway of the fort, A Famosa; the Portuguese fortifications were subsequently demolished by the British. Nevertheless, there is a small Roman Catholic Eurasian community in Malacca that traces its roots back to the early Portuguese settlers and retains some modified elements of their language and culture, and A Famosa is an essential part of every guided tour of the town. The Portuguese also erected a church in the center of the town and named it "Our Lady of the Hill." Subsequently it became a Dutch burial ground and was renamed St. Paul's Church.

The Dutch

The Portuguese held Malacca for well over a century, but suffered continuous harassment from other surrounding Muslim states, including Aceh in northern Sumatra and nearby Johor where the exiled Sultan and his retinue reestablished themselves. Eventually the Portuguese succumbed to the emerging mercantile and naval power of the Dutch, and from their base in Java and with support from the Sultan of Johor the Dutch took control of Malacca in 1641. For more than a century the Dutch reigned supreme in the archipelago and enforced trade monopolies on spices. During this time Malacca languished while the Dutch focused on their main settlement of Batavia (later Jakarta) in western Java; in alliance with the Dutch, the sultanate of Johor also prospered. Nevertheless, the Dutch left an indelible imprint on central Malacca in the shape of the Dutch governor's residence (*stadhuys*), built in 1650, and Christ Church, erected in 1753.

The British and the Straits Settlements

The center of political and economic gravity again shifted when the English East India Company secured the agreement of the Sultan of Kedah, well to the north of Malacca, to establish a base on the large west coast island of Penang (Pulau Pinang) in 1786. The British had built up their power in India, and were concerned to protect their interests there and in the expanding India-China trade by establishing a presence on the eastern margins of the Bay of Bengal. Francis Light named Penang Prince of Wales Island and the British settlement there George Town. A coastal mainland strip opposite the island (subsequently named Province Wellesley) was also transferred to Britain by the

Sultan of Kedah in 1800. The British position on the Malayan Peninsula was further consolidated with the founding of Singapore by Thomas Stamford Raffles in 1819 and the eventual transfer of Malacca to the British by the terms of the Anglo-Dutch Treaty of London in 1824. All these settlements were brought together in 1826 as the Straits Settlements and administered from British India and then from the Colonial Office in London in 1867. As port centers Penang, Malacca, and Singapore were characterized by their cosmopolitan populations; they attracted traders and migrants from all over Asia and from the Middle East. In particular they all became important destinations for southern Chinese settlement.

The British and the Malay States

From their trading bases on the fringes of the Malay world the British were subsequently drawn into the affairs of the Malayan hinterland when tin mining expanded rapidly on the basis of finance and southern Chinese coolie labor organized through the Straits Settlements. Increasing conflicts between rival Chinese secret societies for control of the rich tin fields, particularly in the regions of Larut and Kinta in the state of Perak, not far from Penang, and the inability of the Malay sultan and his territorial chiefs to maintain law and order there inevitably led to British intervention. Taking advantage of a succession dispute in the Perak sultanate, the

British concluded a treaty, the Pangkor Engagement, with their favored candidate in 1874 by which a British Resident and supporting officials were installed to "advise" the Sultan. Similar agreements were reached with the other tin states of Selangor and Negeri Sembilan, and subsequently in 1888 a British Resident was installed in Pahang. These four states were then brought into a consolidated federal relationship in 1896 and administered from the new capital of the federation, Kuala Lumpur, a rapidly growing tin-mining town situated at the confluence of the Klang and Gombak Rivers.

The wealth of these western regions of the peninsula was based initially on rich tin deposits, but the economy was augmented significantly with the development of rubber cultivation and the rapid expansion of mainly foreign-owned rubber estates, worked primarily by immigrant south Indian Tamil labor, as well as the rapid increase in local, mainly Malay, rubber gardens grown on small farms. To service this fast-expanding colonial economy the British also developed a road, railway, and port infrastructure.

Most of the remaining Malay States (Kedah, Perlis, Terengganu, Kelantan), which were then under Siamese suzerainty, were progressively brought into the British colonial system and in 1909 as protected and unfederated territories the Sultans there were also assigned British officers. Johor was the last state to be assigned an adviser in 1914.

Britain and Northern Borneo

In the Borneo territories there was a similarly piecemeal British approach to the extension of power. In Sarawak, the English adventurer James Brooke, and then his nephew Charles, as Rajahs recognized by the Brunei sultans, gradually extended their domains through cession and annexation at the expense of Brunei. In return for putting down a local rebellion against Brunei, James Brooke was appointed Rajah and Governor of Sarawak in November 1841. At that time the state only occupied a relatively small corner of northwestern Borneo, but James embarked on ambitious plans for expansion. By the early twentieth century piracy and tribal head-hunting had been suppressed and the Sarawak domains of Charles Brooke were extensive and had completely surrounded the small and weakened Brunei sultanate. In addition in the late 1870s a British businessman, Alfred Dent, went into partnership with the Austrian Consul in Hong Kong and secured territories in the northeastern regions of Borneo from the Sultans of Brunei and Sulu. The British government gave Dent's company a royal charter in 1881, and henceforth the British North Borneo Chartered Company, like the Brooke Raj to the south, began to extend its possessions and progressively took over the administration of territories to the northwest of

Sarawak and Brunei and to the south of the Philippines. Sarawak, British North Borneo, and Brunei were granted Protectorate status by the British in 1888 to ensure that this region remained firmly in British hands.

The British Legacy and the Plural Society

Overall Britain created a colonial economy in these disparate territories, which were progressively integrated into the British Empire and the world market. Malaya in particular became a major exporter of tin and natural rubber. Subsequently oil was discovered in Sarawak and neighboring Brunei. One of the most significant, and for postindependence Malaysia, worrying legacies of the colonial period was the creation of a culturally diverse set of communities, generated principally by large-scale immigration from other parts of Asia.

The broad ethnic categories today recognized in Malaysia—the Malays, the Chinese, and the Indians, along with minority groups in peninsular Malaysia, lumped together as *orang asli*, or aborigines, and in the Borneo territories, the indigenous Dayaks—became closely, though not completely, associated with economic functions during the colonial period. Malays tended to be involved in traditional peasant and small farm agriculture and fishing, though there were those who were also drawn into the colonial administration and were employed in the sultanates. Traditional Malay culture and

communities thrived particularly in the remoter east-coast peninsular states of Kelantan and Terengganu and away from the main centers of commerce. The Chinese were drawn into the colonial economy as entrepreneurs and wage laborers, and were important intermediaries in trade, retailing, and finance, especially in the more developed, economically active west-coast states and in the urban areas of the peninsula. Indians moved into urban-based occupations in shopkeeping, trade, moneylending, the police, army, and professions, and Tamils from southern India were employed as laborers on rubber plantations. A more complex, but nevertheless broadly similar plural system developed in the Borneo territories as well.

The Last Years of Colonialism
The Interwar Years
Although Malaysia did not see the strongly anticolonial nationalist movements that developed in other parts of Southeast Asia, there was an increasing consciousness of identity among the three major ethnic categories of Chinese, Indians, and Malays. The Chinese and Indians in particular were influenced by the emerging nationalisms in their home countries, and the Malays responded to the perceived threat of being swamped by the

culturally very different and economically more successful Chinese and, to a lesser extent, Indians. The Borneo territories saw very little in the way of organized anticolonial protest.

The Japanese Occupation

The rapid Japanese invasion and conquest of Southeast Asia between December 1941 and February 1942 took the Western colonial powers by surprise. It demonstrated that the assumptions of the local populations about the invincibility of the West and the permanence and power of colonialism were mistaken. Just over three years of Japanese occupation and the disruption of war also paved the way for indigenous nationalist movements and political leaders to declare or secure political independence

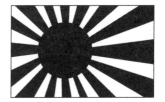

in the immediate postwar years in North Vietnam, Burma, Indonesia, and the Philippines. In Malaysia nationalist sentiments, while present, did not result in a united struggle for independence, given the sharp ethnic divisions and Britain's intention to grant independence sooner rather than later.

The Prelude to Independence

In Sarawak and British North Borneo events took a rather different turn. The damage inflicted by war and occupation meant that the Brookes in Sarawak and the Chartered Company in British

North Borneo could no longer muster the resources to administer their respective territories in a rapidly changing and far more politically unstable and uncertain postwar world. The internal administration of both protectorates was therefore taken over by the British government and they were designated as crown colonies.

In the Malayan Peninsula Britain formulated plans to bring the disparate Malayan territories (with the exception of Singapore) together as a crown colony called the Malayan Union in 1946. This was designed to give all peoples, local and immigrant, equal citizenship rights, and, had it been implemented, it would also have served to weaken the special position of the Malays and the Sultans. Quite naturally this provoked strong opposition from the Malays; it served as a spur to their political coordination, and it resulted in a British climbdown, and the decision to replace the Union with the Federation of Malaya and to acknowledge and confirm the special position of the Malays *vis-à-vis* the immigrant populations, particularly the Chinese.

Ethnic divisions emerged forcefully with a most traumatic experience for postwar Malaya. The so-called Malayan Emergency was instigated by a largely Chinese anti-Japanese military force, dominated by the Malayan Communist Party, which went back into the jungle to fight for independence from Britain. The young disaffected Chinese, though fighting for independence, as they had done during the Japanese occupation, were also fighting, as they saw it, for the rights of all Malayans. The Emergency lasted from 1948 until 1960, during which time the British worked and negotiated with a pro-British alliance of ethnic-based Malay (United Malays National Organization [UMNO]), Chinese (Malayan Chinese Association [MCA]), and Indian (Malayan Indian Congress [MIC]) political parties led by Tunku Abdul Rahman, which carried the Federation of Malaya (comprising the Federated and Unfederated Malay States, Malacca, and Penang) into independence on August 31, 1957. The Tunku, a member of the Kedah royal family, and an enormously respected political leader, became the first prime minister of an independent Malaya.

Malaysian Independence

The wider Federation of Malaysia came into being on August 31, 1963, with the addition of Singapore, Sarawak, and Sabah. Political differences over ethnic representation and rights between the Malay-dominated government in Kuala Lumpur and Chinese-dominated Singapore resulted in Singapore's departure from the Federation in 1965 and the establishment of a separate Singapore Republic. The Sultan of Brunei declined to join the Federation, following extended and difficult negotiations over his status *vis-à-vis* other Malay sultans and over rights to

Brunei's oil revenue; Brunei eventually reached agreement to end its protected status and was granted full independence from Britain on January 1, 1984.

Since the independence of Malaya in 1957 and the enlargement of the Federation to form Malaysia in 1963, the country has been governed by a Malay-dominated coalition, primarily through UMNO. All of the country's five Prime Ministers have come from this Malay party.

GOVERNMENT

Malaysia is an unusual example of a federal constitutional monarchy that is also the product of the rather ad hoc arrangements that Britain put in place to ensure convenient and effective administration and economic development. It has nine potential kings and therefore nine royal families—truly an abundance of royalty. The nine hereditary sultans of the former Federated and Unfederated Malay states take it in turns, once every five years, to serve as the elected King of Malaysia, styled the *Yang di-Pertuan Agong*. The Conference of Rulers elects one among their number to succeed. The remaining states of Penang and Malacca, formerly part of the British

Straits Settlements, and Sarawak and Sabah, which were crown colonies, have governors appointed by the government for a four-year period, and do not participate in royal selection.

Malaysia is also an electoral democracy on the model of the Westminster parliamentary system, with a lower house, the elected House of Representatives (*Dewan Rakyat*), and a partly appointed Senate as the upper house (*Dewan Negara*). Yet, in spite of a vigorous electoral system with regular elections and colorful electioneering, the country since independence has been governed by a Malay-dominated alliance of mainly ethnic-based parties. More power is embodied in the executive branch of government than the legislative branch, and the judiciary is closely controlled.

As a federation, the government comprises both federal and state-level institutions and organs. As with its royalty, Malaysia also has an abundance of government and administration. Malaysians are federal citizens, except for the East Malaysian territories, where they are citizens distinguished in various ways from their peninsular cousins. All citizens must carry an identity card from twelve years of age. There are also three federal territories: Kuala Lumpur, Putrajaya, and Labuan. Each state has its own legislative chamber (*Dewan Undangan Negeri*) led by a chief minister who is referred to as a

Menteri Besar in the Malay States and a *Ketua Menteri* in the four states with nonhereditary rulers or governors. Every state capital will usually have a harmonious mix of federal and state institutions, often occupying grand high-rise buildings.

ECONOMIC DEVELOPMENT AND ETHNICITY

The special position of the Malays in Malaysia and the need to provide them with a measure of protection against the more economically successful Chinese has been the major issue to dominate postindependence political life. There has been constant concern about issues to do with "race" or ethnicity, which are very sensitive matters in the country. Things came to a head with the postelection "race riots" and Malay–Chinese conflict on May 13, 1969. A state of emergency was declared and the then deputy prime minister, Tun Abdul Razak, took over a National Operations Council to promote national unity and ensure political stability. He then became the second prime minister following Tunku Abdul Rahman's retirement in September 1970.

The UMNO-led Alliance then formulated its New Economic Policy (NEP), an antipoverty development strategy, directed primarily at addressing Malay poverty, and which sought to remove the identification of "race" with economic function by positive discrimination. The policy also required the achievement of economic growth so that the additional resources made available could be deployed in large part to raise Malay standards of living and to bring the rural Malays in particular into the modern sector, industry, and commerce without unduly penalizing the Chinese. Employment quotas in the public sector, scholarships for higher education, specific requirements for investment and ownership of companies, and regulations governing public contracts and licenses were all designed to shift the balance toward the Malays. The NEP, which necessarily required an expanded and interventionist role for the state, was instituted in the Second Malaysia (Development) Plan of 1971–75. Malaysia also embarked on a strategy of export-oriented industrialization and actively sought foreign direct investment. This policy was continued under Malaysia's third Prime Minister, Dato Hussein Onn, who took office in January 1976.

Despite some ups and downs, particularly the Asian financial crisis of 1997–98, the Malaysian economy has modernized and industrialized. These achievements accelerated under Malaysia's fourth prime minister, Tun Dr Mahathir Mohamad, who came to power in 1981. The longest-serving Prime Minister, Tun Mahathir set his country the ambitious task of achieving fully industrialized and developed status by the year 2020. The positive discrimination in favor of the Malays, though this policy has been softened in recent years, and the success in achieving economic growth, have managed to secure political stability, a degree of interethnic harmony and acceptance, and unprecedented prosperity for an increasing number of citizens.

With industrialization, Malaysia now has its own successful multinational companies, none more important than the Malaysian National Oil Company, Petronas (Petronui Nasional Berhad); the Malaysian government also engineered through the stock market the takeover of large

British-owned multinational companies, particularly in the plantation, trading, and services sectors. In the 1990s the country embarked on several megaprojects. The high-rise landscape of Kuala Lumpur boasts one of the tallest buildings in the world, the Petronas twin towers, and the majestic Menara KL Tower; there has been frenzied development of new residential, industrial, and "high-tech" zones, such as Cyberjaya in the Klang Valley; high-rise office, hotel, and apartment complexes line the main expressway from the airport to the capital; the road, rail, airport, and telecommunications infrastructure has been expanded and upgraded; there is the new Kuala Lumpur International Airport at Subang with an Express Rail link to KL. The Formula One racing circuit at Sepang, which has secured agreement for F1 Grand Prix until

2015, and the Light Rail Transit system in KL speak of a modern, globalized nation; there is a new administrative capital, Putrajaya, near the airport. Malaysia, from a predominantly rural and agricultural society in the mid-twentieth century, has become increasingly urbanized. The new images are of young Malaysians in designer jeans, with the ubiquitous mobile phones, shopping in air-conditioned malls or sitting in traffic jams.

Tun Mahathir retired in 2003, and bequeathed this successfully modernizing country to his successor, Datuk Seri Abdullah Badawi. But what strikes the observer of Malaysian affairs over the past forty years is the rapidity of this social and economic transformation, which shows no sign of slowing down and which the current prime minister has to attempt to administer and control.

Two areas of Malaysian life are of particular interest and concern at the beginning of the twenty-first century: first, the changing values and lifestyles of young Malaysians, the impact of globalization on the traditional cultures, and how new and old can be brought into a harmonious relationship; and second, the pressures that are bearing down on the environment because of the

demands of the modern middle-class consumer for cars, commodities, leisure, and travel.

VALUES & ATTITUDES

A CULTURAL POTPOURRI

Malaysia is most decidedly a plural society:
multiethnic, multilingual, and multicultural.
Before exploring this diversity, however, it may be
useful to emphasize the overriding character of the
country. Malaysian national identity is based on
the major elements of indigenous Malay culture.

The national language is
Malay. The state religion
is Islam, though with
freedom of worship for
the country's Buddhists,
Confucians/Taoists,
Hindus, Sikhs, and
Christians. The king is a
Malay sultan, and the
Prime Minister is always Malay. Malays are
dominant in the main public sector national
institutions such as government, the bureaucracy,
and the police and military.

As we have seen, traditionally the Malays were
rural-based, small-scale farmers, fishermen, and
traders; many of them also served as administrators
in the Malay states. In popular tourist images the

Malays are depicted in idyllic villages, living in thatched and wooden houses that are raised on stilts, shaded by coconut palms, sometimes on wide, sandy beaches; they wear large woven sun hats while they plow their paddies using buffalo, and transplant and harvest their rice in picturesque landscapes. They are seen flying colorful paper kites, spinning tops, and kicking woven rattan balls. However, these popular and stereotypical representations disguise a different reality. A rapidly growing urban, educated Malay middle class has emerged, though largely concentrated in the public sector, and Malays generally have become more urbanized. Those still in the countryside have embraced commercial agriculture.

The Chinese are mainly in private business, commerce, industry, and the professions. Their presence is obvious in the central business districts and markets of the main towns and cities. A popular image is the Chinese shopkeeper, usually referred to as *towkay*, in vest, shorts, and sandals, sitting at the front of his shop house with wares displayed on the adjacent sidewalk under the cool covered walkway. However, the Chinese are also found in commercial agriculture, such as in market gardening near urban areas. Many were also tin miners, though now there are only small numbers

employed in the mining sector, and many work in industry, construction, the professions, and the service sector. Tourist literature frequently refers to the diverse, colorful, and noisy Chinese markets and stalls selling everything from cooked food, fruit, vegetables, flowers, fish, meat, designer items (clothes, watches, shoes, jewelry, perfumes), handicrafts (not just Chinese items), and souvenirs. Chinese lion and dragon dances, temples, Chinese opera, Buddhist statuary, lanterns, paper money and scrolls, fireworks and rockets, and joss sticks are again part of the cultural paraphernalia and touristic representation of the Chinese community.

The Indians are located predominantly in the urban sector in the professions, urban retailing, police, and army. The tourist will come across Indian money changers, who dominate the sector. Some continue to work in rural areas as estate laborers. Images of Hindu temples and rituals, street hawkers, colorful textile shops, and curry houses abound.

Many of the *orang asli* and Dayaks are still found in the interior regions of the peninsula, Sarawak, and Sabah as farmers. Some work on public sector plantations and in the timber industry. Increasingly younger people are finding their way into urban centers working in government, the public sector, and service industries. However, again the images that depict them may be rather different. One of the most striking is the tattooed Iban warrior in a loincloth, with hornbill feather headdress, beads, silver jewelry, arm- and leg-bands, and carrying a head-hunting sword or a blowpipe and shield. The foreign visitor should be aware of the difference between popular images and reality, and the fact that modern and traditional values intermingle.

Of course, generalizations about Malaysian society are just that, and they may not hold in all instances. There are always exceptions, and it is best to think of values as expressing particular emphases and tendencies. Do not expect Malaysians always to behave in a particular way, and keep in mind that as an ethnically diverse country, there will always be variations in behavior between different groups, as we shall see in the later discussion of business relationships in particular. Even within the same ethnic grouping, say the Malays, there are also younger and older Malays, men and women, and those of different social class, and occupational and educational backgrounds. The core, or "traditional," Malaysian values and attitudes discussed below have been subject to external influences. Western or modern values and interests disseminated through the popular media, film, television, music, education, and the Internet and through contact with Western businesspeople, tourists, and travelers have made an impact particularly among the younger generation and the urban population.

FAMILY

Let us now look for some common threads in this cultural pluralism. For Malaysians of all ethnic groups the values of family and kinship continue to be relatively strong, though among the younger generation there is a tendency for these to weaken with the pace of modernization and globalization and the physical and social mobility that goes with it. Obviously it is more difficult for urban Malaysians, and particularly urban Malays, to keep in touch with family in rural areas, though they still do their best. During major festivals and holidays one often hears the phrase *balik kampung* used among the Malay community; they are "returning to their village" to reunite with their family even if what they are returning to is not quite a village, or no longer as rural as it once was.

Family membership provides an individual with support, security, identity, and status, though one is expected to discharge one's responsibilities and obligations in return. Malaysians remain very family-oriented, and family matters and interests take priority over other relationships. Families spend time together: a common sight in the early evening is that of local families, including children and grandparents, eating together in restaurants.

Malaysians take great pride in their children, who are lavished with affection, protected, petted, and indulged by parents and senior relatives. Adoption is quite widely practiced within kinship circles, especially among Malays and Dayaks.

Generally, women are more closely associated with housekeeping, child

rearing, and the domestic sphere, and men with the public sphere. In Chinese and Indian societies, inequality between men and women is noticeable, and in Muslim societies a degree of segregation of the sexes is evident in social gatherings. Nevertheless, there is a degree of flexibility in these relationships, and there are many examples of young fathers helping with child rearing, shopping, and domestic tasks; women are increasingly pursuing higher education and careers outside the home; and middle-class working women frequently employ domestic help. Moreover, women in Malaysia, as in Southeast Asia generally, traditionally played significant roles in rural economies, in agriculture, handicraft industries, and small-scale retailing. They are well-known for their astuteness in financial affairs.

CONFORMITY AND HARMONY

It follows from the strong sense of social and familial solidarity and responsibility that in Malaysia individual interests tend to be subordinated to the needs of the wider social group. In this situation deviation from social norms is difficult. There is therefore a higher degree of conformity than in Western societies, participation in community life is greatly valued, and mutual reciprocity is encouraged.

Social harmony is another important element of this ethos. Many Malaysians believe strongly that good relations within the community should be maintained, and that the behavior, morality, and spiritual condition of each person influence others. These attitudes place emphasis on the importance of consensus. Time has to be devoted to consultation with family, colleagues, and friends, and to collective decision making in a calm, controlled, and cooperative atmosphere. Openly expressed anger, aggression, or impatience directed at an individual is frowned upon, and is highly inappropriate.

DEFERENCE AND RESPECT

The family is in one sense a unit held together by bonds of affection, trust, support, obligation, and solidarity. But it also embodies and defines another social principle that is pervasive in Malaysian society, and that is hierarchy, or inequality, and the associated attitudes of deference and respect. The head of the family is usually the senior male, and relations are ranked according to relative age and seniority. Parents nurture, support, socialize, and protect their children, and other family members are usually on call to help when needed in return for the respect and loyalty demanded of their juniors. An older brother or sister may have to assume some responsibility for younger siblings, such as paying towards their education or assisting in the development of their careers. Children are expected to care for their parents in old age.

Among the Chinese the importance of the patriarchal extended family has also been sustained, and it is still evident in family business organization based on kinship, loyalty, and subservience, and the fact that everyone knows their place. However, even here there have been changes in the degree to which kinship bonds still matter in Chinese business circles, as we shall see later.

CONSENSUS

Malaysians love meetings, and the group ethic also finds its expression in traditional Malay village communities, with their emphasis on mutual cooperation (*gotong royong*) and consensus (*muafakat*) through meeting and discussion (*mesyuarat*). Direct confrontation and vigorous debate with strongly held opposing views are usually avoided; instead styles of communication tend toward obliqueness, vagueness, and subtlety in attempts to overcome potential conflict. We return to this issue in Chapter 8.

FACE

Westerners are familiar with the notion of "losing face." It is an even more important concept in Malaysian society. It has to do with a person's identity, self-respect, and honor, and it also involves an evaluation or judgment by others in the context of a strong familial and community ethos. What others think of you matters. An individual can even lose face if someone close to them—a son, daughter, or sibling, for example—

behaves inappropriately or comes in for criticism or gossip from others.

ATTITUDES TO FOREIGNERS
Politeness

In keeping with the Malaysian emphasis on social harmony, control, and respect, and the fact that Malaysians live in a long-established multicultural environment in which they have had to live and work together with those of different cultures and ethnicities, the foreign visitor will find that, in general, their hosts are welcoming, tolerant, and polite. If the outsider is well behaved, is prepared to adapt and to interact with local people on their terms, and shows an interest in the local culture and language, then Malaysians will reciprocate in a helpful and friendly manner, though, of course, you should beware the over-friendly tout or huckster in tourist areas. If you are not so well behaved, you will not usually be reprimanded; rather you will receive cool, distant, but still polite service and responses, though you are already marked out as a "stupid" or "crass" foreigner rather than a "nice" one, and you will not have earned respect. Until you get to know them Malaysians are unlikely to correct you or to tell you to your face that you are doing something inappropriately; this would cause embarrassment to them and to you. However, if you ask for advice and guidance, it will be politely given.

One of the Family

Affectionate family feelings, and the obligations that go with them, may be extended to others. As you get to know Malaysians you may find that they attempt to draw you into their circle by addressing you with a kinship term such as "brother," "sister," "aunt," or "uncle." You will have made friends for life, and the kinship bonds persist through time, even without regular face-to-face contact.

Personal Questions

In particular, and in a polite way, Malaysians will often ask foreign visitors about their family circumstances. They may ask whether or not you are married, and especially whether or not you have children, and ask about other matters to do with your social standing, occupation, and background. This should not be interpreted as undue prying: Malaysians are genuinely interested in getting to know you and finding out what kind of person you are, and it is seen as good manners to do so. This also helps your hosts in framing their social behavior and interaction with you. The best way to address this is to respond politely, ask them about their circumstances as well, and show an interest in their position within their society. This kind of exchange gives valuable topics for conversation and helps to break the ice.

Avoiding Public Embarrassment

The crucial principle in adapting to Malaysian cultural ways is to avoid public embarrassment.

Openly displaying what you think or feel is not appreciated in Malaysia. If you deliver a public reprimand for what you consider to be poor service in a restaurant or shop, or for what you think to be inappropriate or rude behavior, it will usually go down very badly and will not necessarily achieve your desired objective. The rather blunt remark that a Western visitor might make in a casual conversation should also be avoided. For the business visitor to Malaysia, and for the expatriate working there, the diplomatic and sensitive handling of relationships and exchanges is vitally important (see Chapter 8).

HUMOR

Malaysians have a developed sense of humor, but it is best to wait until you get to know them well before plunging in with your favorite jokes. Local humor is primarily visual and ranges from slapstick to the coarse, though usually among close friends and family. Irony is used as a comic device as well as for poking fun at those with pretensions. You should be prepared to laugh at yourself, particularly if you make a cultural gaffe. Malaysians will not usually laugh outright at this, but they will smile if you show that you are not overly embarrassed and are prepared to learn from your mistake.

Subtle and polished verbal humor demands a considerable command of the local language, so don't try it unless you are confident in the Malaysian language. But you must be very cautious about using any ethnic-based or political jokes in Malaysia's multicultural society, or sexual innuendo in mixed male-female company, and especially in the company of devout Muslims. Don't tell jokes that could embarrass your host or cause him to lose face. A good way to get into local humor is to read the local newspapers and cartoons.

FLEXIBLE TIME

The Malaysian preoccupation with keeping the family and social relations in good order, ensuring consensus, and maintaining harmony, requires time. The concept of Malaysian time is generally more flexible and open-ended than in the West; it is sometimes referred to locally as "rubber time," in that it can be stretched and molded. Malaysians will endeavor to be punctual, but there may well be more pressing matters. Don't be surprised if you are given a broad time span within which your meeting will take place, or if it overruns.

THINKING OF OTHERS

Overall, then, the foreign visitor should be conscious of the fact that Malaysian life is governed by social and community considerations, and by being aware, at all times, of the feelings of others. Everyday encounters and interactions require you to put a lot of effort and thought into conscientiously putting yourself into the other person's shoes.

chapter three

RELIGION
& FESTIVALS

Given their rich cultural mix, Malaysians always seem to be celebrating something, and though they usually invite members of other ethnic groups to some of their major festivals, their rituals are one of the clearest expressions of ethnic difference. Visitors used to the more secular societies of the West will soon realize that they are moving in a more religiously and spiritually charged and meaningful environment, and that mosques, temples, and churches are actively used and central parts of the lives of Malaysians.

The Malaysians enjoy several different religious festivals and public holidays. A small number of these are fixed. However, Muslim, Chinese, and Hindu calendars are lunar ones, and therefore years are not of the same length, and the dates of most Malaysian celebrations are variable. The constituent states also have their own holidays, usually to celebrate such events as the local Sultan's or Governor's birthday, and not all events have religious significance. Visitors should check at the offices of Tourism Malaysia (Malaysia Tourism Promotion Board), or the Sarawak or Sabah Tourism Boards for further information.

Major celebrations are publicized in promotional literature, in the press, and on television.

> **MAJOR PUBLIC HOLIDAYS AND FESTIVALS**
>
> New Year (not celebrated in all states) **January 1**
>
> Chinese New Year **late January–February**
>
> Hari Raya Puasa (Breaking of the Muslim Fast) **variable date**
>
> Vesak Day (the Buddha's Birthday) **April–May**
>
> Worker's Day or Labor Day **May 1**
>
> King's Official Birthday **first Saturday in June**
>
> National Day or Independence Day **August 31**
>
> Deepavali (Festival of Lights) **October–November**
>
> Christmas Day **December 25**

Some festivals have variable dates and are specific to particular ethnic groups: Hari Raya Haji (marking the successful conclusion of the pilgrimage to Mecca); Muslim New Year (Awal Muharam); the Prophet's Birthday (Maulud Nabi); the Muslim Fasting Month of Ramadan, or Puasa; and the Buddhist celebration of the Buddha's birthday (Vesak Day); there is also the Hindu Indian festival of Thaipusam in January–February.

Then there are celebrations for specific purposes: Federal Territory Day (in Kuala Lumpur, Labuan, and Putrajaya), February 1; Kaamatan Festival (Harvest Festival, Sabah and Labuan), May 30–31; Gawai Dayak (Harvest Festival, Sarawak), June 1–2; the Chinese Hungry Ghosts Festival, usually in July–August, and the Moon Cake Festival, September–early October.

Every religion also has rites of passage or transition that mark important stages of the life cycle: birth, puberty, marriage, and death. In Malaysia these are usually attended by relatives and friends and are seen as ritually significant occasions that demand that those close to the person or persons at the center of the ceremony should attend and fulfill their obligations (reciprocated in due course when those attending organize their own rituals and invite others). A central and underlying principle of ritual activity is that it is based on reciprocity and mutual interest in meeting social and spiritual needs.

MALAYS AND INDIAN MUSLIMS

Malays and Indian Muslims are guided by the five basic principles of Islam: the profession or declaration of one's faith in God and the Prophet; the offering of prayer normally five times a day (at dawn, noon, mid-afternoon, sunset, and after dark); the contribution of *zakat*, an annual charitable tribute or tithe; the observance of the fast or Ramadan (Puasa); and undertaking the pilgrimage to Mecca at least once in one's lifetime.

The most obvious expression of Muslim religious life is Friday prayer, when men go to the mosque *(mesjid)* or the prayer house *(surau)*. Usually they wear a black velvet cap *(songkok)*, which is often worn at work or in the office as well, or a white skullcap or turban if they have undertaken the pilgrimage to Mecca. They may wear a robe in Arab style, with a loose jacket and a *sarung* (a decorated wraparound cloth for the lower body) or a cotton or silk suit with a richly decorated gold brocade *sarung* folded around the waist. The traditional call to prayer was usually issued from the minaret by the *imam*, but today it more frequently booms out as a prerecorded message.

Non-Muslims should not pay sightseeing visits or take photographs at this particular time. However, at other times visitors are welcome to enter a mosque if they are suitably dressed, with men in long trousers and women with arms covered and a long skirt. If you are not wearing appropriate clothing, a cloth or gown to cover yourself will be supplied. Shoes should be removed at the entrance to a mosque, and the visitor should behave in a quiet, controlled, and respectful manner.

Every Muslim home has its copy of the holy book, the Qu'ran, or Koran. It is treated with great respect, and usually kept in a special place covered by a cloth. Hands must be washed before handling it. Visitors, whether to a mosque or a home, should not casually touch the Qu'ran, even in order to learn more about it.

The ability to quote and chant passages from the Qu'ran is highly valued, and many children, both boys and girls, are sent to a Qu'ranic teacher to learn passages by rote.

PHOTOGRAPHY

Most Malaysians like to photograph and be photographed, and as you get to know them you will have no shortage of images and mementoes of your stay.

However, in general it is wise not to take photographs in sacred places or of particular rituals. If you wish to do so, you should ask the custodian's permission. If someone is in the act of prayer, don't disturb them, walk in front of them, or point your camera at them.

Performances staged for tourists are another matter, though these tend to be of a more generally cultural and nonreligious character. In any case it is always polite to ask whether a person minds being photographed.

Ramadan (Puasa)

During Ramadan, the ninth month of the Muslim calendar, believers do not eat, drink, or smoke from sunrise to sunset for twenty-eight or twenty-nine days. Evil thoughts should be banished from the mind and a determined effort made to lead a pure life. It was the time when the Prophet exercised stern self-discipline as a means to cleanse the spirit and the body. During this time it would be less than tactful to eat, drink, or offer refreshments in the presence of those who are fasting. It would also be inappropriate to ask someone if they are fasting (which implies that you think they might not be), and it is best not to visit them socially or call in casually during the day. The household routine is transformed, with family meals being prepared very early in the morning and late at night. At this time some people find it difficult to carry out a demanding job or energetic sports, particularly as the day wears on. Certain people, such as the elderly and infirm, young children, and pregnant or menstruating women, are not required to fast.

The end of the fasting month is called Hari Raya, or Hari Raya Puasa. Special prayers are offered at the mosque and an open house is held for family, friends, neighbors, and colleagues. It is the one event in the Muslim calendar to which a foreign visitor might be invited. Celebrations usually last for three days. It is a time for visiting and giving special thanks to parents and other senior relatives, and asking for forgiveness for past sins. Invitations are by word of mouth or a formal card, but a visitor can usually go along with a friend because open house means what it says. However, the times during which you can visit will be specified. Some houses will open for most of the day, but if

you receive an invitation to the house of a dignitary, dates and times will be more precisely specified. It is an opportunity to sample the best of

Malay or Indian curries, relishes, fish, and varieties of cooked rice. Do so sparingly if you have many houses on your itinerary.

This is an appropriate time to redecorate or refurbish the house, and people put up colored lights, bunting, and tinsel. They may make or buy new clothes at this time, and everyone dresses in their best. Men don their *songkok* with brightly colored cotton or silk suits and richly decorated gold brocaded *sarung*, and women wear the *baju kurung*, a long, decorated, usually batik or gold or silver brocaded dress, with a long-sleeved blouse that reaches to the thighs.

Bringing a gift is not strictly necessary, but it is a nice idea to bring your hosts some flowers, sweetmeats, or candy, and to greet them with "*Selamat* Hari Raya." Generally the recipient of a wrapped gift puts it aside to open later. The modest and thankful receipt of a gift and the thought behind it are what is important, not so much what is in the package.

The exact timing of the celebrations depends on the sighting of the New Moon at the end of the month, and is then pronounced officially in the media. If the moon is not sighted on the last night of the month the breaking of the fast may be postponed for a further day. Everything shuts down for Hari Raya eve and the next couple of days. The reuniting of family and friends means that airports, railway stations, bus terminals, and roads are crammed with people returning to their home communities. Traffic jams out of Kuala

Lumpur and other major cities and towns are legendary. Usually transportation facilities, especially domestic flights, are block-booked several months in advance, and hotel and other accommodation can be a problem.

It is well to remember that there is another Hari Raya for Muslims, referred to as Hari Raya Haji, which marks the successful completion of the pilgrimage to Mecca. In such states as Kelantan and Terengganu there is a two-day holiday with much feasting and celebration on the return of the honored pilgrims, although in general it is not as lavishly celebrated in Malaysia as it is in the Middle East. For Malaysia Hari Raya Puasa is the main calendrical event. However, one may well see returning Muslims at airports and transport terminals adorned in Middle Eastern and Arab dress—a sure sign that they have been to Saudi Arabia and that they are openly expressing that important occasion.

Weddings

For the foreign visitor, Muslim wedding ceremonies (particularly Malay weddings) are of more importance than other rites of passage because of the greater likelihood of being invited to at least part of the celebrations. They are colorful affairs and, if you are invited to one, you should accept without hesitation.

In past times marriages were arranged by the senior members of the two families, and this may still happen from time to time, though less formally. Marriages today are generally much more a matter of personal choice, though parents will normally be consulted and the two families will decide on the details of the wedding and how the expenses are to be shared. Traditionally the wedding is held in the bride's home and the groom is conducted there in procession, bearing gifts, and accompanied by tambourines, drums, and singing.

Customs may vary from region to region and can depend on whether the ceremony is held in an urban or rural setting. Bride and groom usually wear richly decorated silk brocade costumes, and the bride is also adorned with an array of traditional Malay gold and silver ornament. The groom and his family usually pay for the bride's costume, and the groom is expected to buy his bride personal gifts such as perfumes and jewelry. The first part of the ceremony consists of a declaration by the groom to the bride's father of his intention to marry, which he must deliver in the presence of witnesses and Muslim officials. Marriage documents must then be signed. The main element of the wedding for the guests, apart from the food, is the *bersanding* (the sitting-in-state, or enthronement). This is the part of the ceremony that you, as a foreign visitor, are most likely to be invited.

During the *bersanding*, the bride and groom sit quietly and sedately side-by-side on decorated chairs on a raised dais, or on a richly decorated divan or bed. They are not permitted to look at one another, and must remain still and unresponsive to those around them, with eyes lowered. (At a village wedding, where everyone knows one another well, there may be some relaxation, with attempts to distract the couple with bawdy jokes.) Senior family members and friends come forward one by one to bless the couple. This is the solemnization of the marriage.

Honored guests, usually including foreign visitors, are often invited to participate in the *tepong tawar* ritual, first for the groom, then for the bride. The senior women will take you through the ritual. The guests in turn touch the groom's forehead with a gold ring, then a dab of rice flour or scented sandalwood paste is placed there, and his head and hands are lightly scattered with scented flower petals (*bunga rumpai*) and/or saffron rice grains, starting with his right hand and finishing with his left. The bride then goes through the same process. Perfumed water may be sprayed over the couple.

After the *bersanding* the bride and groom turn to each other and feed each other by hand with morsels of sweetened, glutinous rice. The wedding feast then commences. The food may be provided in an informal buffet style, with men and women mixing and sitting together. In a more traditional wedding men and women are seated in separate groups in a prearranged setting, in which case you will be shown to your table. Bride and groom may circulate among the guests. On departure guests are usually given a decorated hard-boiled egg in a small container (*bunga telur*) or sweets or chocolates shaped like eggs to symbolize fertility.

Increasingly in modern, often urban weddings special caterers are employed to provide the food and may also supply costumes and other ritual necessities for rental. The venue might be a hotel or restaurant rather than a domestic setting.

If you are invited to a Muslim wedding, you can send a gift of money in a wedding card or some useful household item in advance to the bride's home, or discreetly present it to a member of the family, usually a parent or an uncle, as they stand in line to greet the guests on the day.

Birth
The casual foreign visitor is unlikely to be invited to attend the ceremonies surrounding birth. However, for the longer established expatriate there may be the opportunity to attend certain of the subsequent ceremonies, though these are primarily religious in nature and so invitations to non-Muslims are unlikely. If an invitation is received then suitable dress, with the body appropriately covered, should be worn. Traditionally after the birth the mother and baby undergo a period of confinement and remain in

the house for around six weeks, during which time the mother eats a special diet and is massaged. Visitors may call briefly during this time to offer congratulations and give their best wishes and flowers or small gifts to the mother and/or baby; or perhaps a discreet gift of money for the child's future. In some cases the ending of this period may be marked by a family ceremony. After this the mother may return to work and assume her normal responsibilities.

Again traditionally there were religious ceremonies in Malay society to introduce the baby to his cradle, to cleanse the baby by head shaving, and finally to place the baby's feet on the ground for the first time. With modernization and urbanization many of these ceremonies might be omitted and the confinement period of the mother and child reduced.

Circumcision
Malay boys are usually circumcised before their teens; an appropriate time is after they have completed their first full reading of the Qu'ran. Nowadays the minor operation is usually performed in privacy by a doctor, and there may then be a family gathering. The large public ceremonies when several boys were circumcised together are confined to a few rural communities.

Funerals
The foreign visitor is highly unlikely to be invited to a Malay funeral, which is a family affair. If you

have a particular connection with the family you may be invited to express your condolences. Either you will be invited to see the body of the deceased, which is placed in the family house for a short period, or you may remain outside and send your condolences, on a written card or letter, to the bereaved. Prayers are said for three nights following the death and then at certain intervals up to a hundred days after; this constitutes the mourning period. Malay funerals do not normally require wreaths. Usually white or mainly white clothing is worn; women cover their heads. Bright colors should not be worn.

CHINESE

The Chinese are mainly Buddhists, but they also follow Taoist and Confucian precepts. However, we might also characterize their belief system as a "folk religion" oriented specifically to the veneration of ancestors, and to interaction with the spirit world and to a host of deities. The Chinese will also usually have favored temples that they attend regularly, and they often pray to particular gods, some of them ancestral, to which they offer prayers of thanks and from which they seek favors, blessings, and good fortune. Normally you are very welcome to enter a Chinese temple and, if you wish, purchase incense sticks to offer prayers to one of the usually numerous gods and goddesses represented there. You might see some worshipers sitting on the floor shaking a container full of long bamboo oracle sticks, from which eventually one stick will fall; the stick contains a message that is then interpreted by a resident fortune-teller.

Snakes Alive!

If you are sensitive to pungent smoke you might decide not to enter a rather dark space full of aromatic fumes. The atmosphere of the Snake Temple in Penang, a favorite tourist destination, is especially acrid, because the fumes are said to render the numerous snakes kept there somnolent and harmless.

The Chinese celebrate several festivals, and of these there are three important ones that the foreign visitor might experience: New Year; the Feast of the Hungry Ghosts; and the Moon Cake Festival. Chinese festivals are centered on the temples, where worshipers burn incense and present offerings of flowers and fruit, and pray to the appropriate deities. A Chinese household will also often have an altar at home at which offerings and obeisance are made.

Chinese New Year

Chinese New Year, which is usually held in January or February, is not strictly a religious festival; it is celebrated by all Chinese whether they are Buddhist, Taoist, Christian, or inclined more to ancestor worship. All business comes to a standstill. It is a national holiday, and in most states is of two days' duration, though you may find that some Chinese may take a little longer break. The celebrations include street parades and dragon dances. Family reunions are an essential part of the celebrations on the first day; there is a generous quantity of food, with a big family dinner, and many toasts are offered. It is a time when all family members make every effort to attend. There is an open house the following day commencing from

mid-morning and ending late evening, with substantial supplies of alcohol, sweetmeats, and snacks. An ample supply of flowers, incense sticks, candles, and red oranges decorate the family altar, and families visit Buddhist temples. Visitors are greeted with handshakes. On the third or fourth day of the celebrations some families also prepare a special meal of raw fish and finely shredded vegetables.

The Lunar New Year is an auspicious time and guests should not talk about anything that might bring bad luck in the forthcoming year, such as illness, misfortune, and death. There is an opportunity to pay respects to one's elders as well as have fun with plenty of eating, drinking, gambling, and, for the youngsters, setting off firecrackers.

Children, or, more exactly, all nonmarried Chinese, are usually given *ang pow*—red paper envelopes containing money (red is a sign of good fortune). If you are invited to a Chinese home a gift of sweets, flowers, or a bottle of brandy or good alcohol is certainly appreciated. A gift of mandarin oranges is particularly appropriate as a symbol of good fortune.

Hungry Ghosts

The Hungry Ghosts festival usually takes place between July and August. At this time the spirits of the dead are thought to roam the earth, and they must be nourished to prevent them from bringing harm to the living. They are presented with food, and the burning of paper money and other paper gifts. The spirits are also entertained with Chinese operatic performances, and there is much lavish eating and drinking. This festival is especially celebrated among the Penang Chinese.

Moon Cake Festival

The Moon Cake Festival in September or October, which marks the appearance of the Autumn moon and celebrates the defeat of the Mongol dynasty in ancient China, is the occasion for the baking and eating of a rich pastry—the moon cake. The cake is made from bean paste, lotus seed, and sometimes duck egg. Colorful lanterns are lit, incense is burned, and there are family dinners. It is considered an auspicious time for organizing major events such as weddings. The foreign visitor should try moon cake—it's delicious!

Weddings

Ang pow are useful gifts if you have been invited to a Chinese wedding; gifts of appropriate household goods are also welcome. These can be given discreetly to the family reception party. Normally an expatriate guest would be invited to the wedding banquet through a formal invitation written in gold lettering on a red card; you are unlikely to be invited to the wedding ceremony itself, which is usually a family affair. In fact, there are usually two banquets: one hosted by the bride's parents a day or two before the wedding ceremony proper, which is the going-away party, and the other by the groom's parents on the day of the wedding or the day after, which welcomes the bride to her new home. Nowadays the reception is usually held in a restaurant or hotel and no expense is spared. It is customary for newlyweds and parents to go from table to table inviting guests to drink the *yum seng*, or "bottoms up." For those prone to getting tipsy very quickly, beware; *yum sengs* come thick and fast!

Births and Deaths

As with Malay custom, there is usually a period of confinement for mother and baby, though for one month. The end of the confinement may be marked by a ceremony, usually modest, though sometimes more lavish; it also involves purification procedures. With modern urban lifestyles these observations are declining rapidly. Traditionally there were restrictions on when friends could visit the mother and child, but now with more hospital births, family friends and colleagues may visit soon after the birth. Gifts for the mother, including flowers and tonics, are appreciated and for the baby toys and clothes. *Ang pow* is also always welcome.

As for funerals, the most obvious element of the ceremony that the casual foreign visitor might encounter is the procession. The coffin is now usually kept at the funeral parlor for three days to one week, though it could still be kept at home. Visitors at this time in paying their respects would be invited to wave lighted incense-sticks during prayers over the coffin.

The funeral procession, which moves on foot through the streets, is a noisy and eye-catching affair. If you are in a shopping area in a town or city you might hear the clash of cymbals and the beat of drums. People at the head of the procession carry lanterns on poles displaying the name and age of the deceased; banner carriers follow; then musicians, making as much percussive noise as possible to drive away evil spirits. The hearse carries the coffin, flowers, and paper replicas of items to be burned at the graveside and transported to the next world to accompany the spirit of the deceased. Family and friends follow the hearse. They may use rental cars and buses to take them to the burial ground.

Other Chinese Festivals

Chinese and other Buddhists usually celebrate Vesak Day in April or May . This is a national holiday in Malaysia marking the Buddha's birth, enlightenment, and death; it is a solemn occasion, with prayers offered at the temple.

The Dragon Boat Festival, between June and August, celebrates a Chinese saint who preferred to drown rather than be corrupted. Boat races are held in Penang and elsewhere.

The Festival of the Nine Emperor Gods falls in September or October and is the occasion for Chinese operas, processions, and, at some temples, fire-walking ceremonies.

HINDU INDIANS

Hindu Indians follow the ancient scriptures, or Vedas. They worship a Supreme Being, which has many forms and natures; the best-known aspects or manifestations of divinity are Brahma, the creator, Siva, the destroyer, and Vishnu, the preserver. A temple is usually dedicated to a particular deity, though more than one main deity may have a place there, and in any case temples are also home to a large number of minor gods and goddesses. Temples are visited at any time during the week, though Friday is usually for collective prayers. Hindus believe in reincarnation and they hold to a fixed or predestined order of things, which in social and religious terms is embodied in the caste system. Indian households usually have a family altar where an oil lamp is lit and offerings of flowers and fruit are made.

Deepavali (Festival of Lights)

The most well-known of the Hindu Indian celebrations is Deepavali, which usually falls in October or November. It is the time for the gathering of family and friends to celebrate the triumph of good over evil in Hindu mythology, and the victory of Lord Rama over the evil King Ravana, or of Krisna over Asura/Naragasuran. Indian streets, houses, and shops are gaily decorated. Open houses are held and houses are also decorated with colored electric lights or lighted oil lamps, flowers, fruit, and sometimes floor decorations made from colored rice, pulses, and beans. It is a time when the old is swept away and a new beginning ushered in with the hope that good fortune and prosperity will follow. People may take baths sprinkled with scented oils and put on their finest new clothes; children receive gifts, and alms are given to the poor.

Thaipusam

The main Hindu public ceremony is Thaipusam, which is usually held in January or February. It is dedicated as a thanksgiving to Lord Subramaniam (Muruga) for prayers that have been answered, and it celebrates the virtues of courage, fortitude, and endurance. It also expresses penance. The most spectacular, colorful, and dramatic part, much photographed by tourists, is when devotees, who have made a vow during the past year, redeem it by carrying ornamental structures (*kavadi*) attached to their bodies by hooks and

steel spikes that penetrate their flesh. The *kavadi* also contains two small pots of milk, which are used to bathe a statue of Lord Subramaniam. The devotees coat their bodies with holy ash, wear saffron robes, and may insert metal skewers through their cheeks and tongues. Participants go into a state of trance while the procession, with singing, chanting, drumming, and libations, makes its way to a temple or shrine.

In Penang there are usually particular routes used in the street parades and rituals held at the Waterfall Temple, and just to the north of Kuala Lumpur, the magnificent Batu Caves, a major tourist attraction, serve as the ritual focus. Both locations house important Hindu shrines.

Weddings

Indian weddings are similar to Malay ones. They are usually held at the bride's house; bride and groom will also sit in state, and wedding guests sprinkle yellow rice and scented water over them. The wedding feast can be buffet-style or a traditional rural feast where guests are seated on the floor and are served with curries on banana leaves. During the ceremony prayers are offered to the god Ganesh, a coconut is broken with a cleaver (symbolizing prosperity, fertility, and purity), the groom hangs a pendant of gold around the neck of his bride, and the couple walks around a sacred fire. Guests present gifts of cash in a wedding card, or a useful household item.

Births and Deaths

For Hindus, there is a period of confinement after birth of between four and six weeks, but visitors can come to offer congratulations while the mother and child are in the hospital or at home. There is usually a name-giving ceremony halfway through the confinement period.

Funerals among Hindus are a male affair. Family, friends, and colleagues can pay their respects before the cremation. Only men attend the cremation, and the mourning period can last for up to six weeks.

CHRISTIAN DAYAKS AND OTHERS

The Christian populations of Malaysia, comprising some Chinese communities, Eurasians, and the non-Malay indigenous peoples of the peninsula and the

Malaysian Borneo states, follow the Christian calendar, including the Christmas celebrations. Meals accompanying Christian weddings and other receptions are either banquet-style in a restaurant or held at the home of parents or family. Christmas is the time of year for the Christian communities to provide an open house; this conforms to the general Malaysian custom of open house, and it tends to replace the traditional Christmas family meal. Christmas Eve is reserved for Midnight Mass, which is followed by a family supper. Obviously the religious element of the wedding is conducted in church or chapel. There are also Easter celebrations and observances; one of the most important is held at St. Peter's Church in Malacca.

In Sarawak the native celebration of *Gawai Dayak* takes place in early June, when there is much feasting and drinking, including spirit and beer made from rice and palm wine. Dancing and cultural performances are held in local longhouses decorated with flags and woven cloths. In effect, it marks the end of the agricultural year with the completion of the rice harvest and a thanksgiving to gods and spirits. In Sabah the equivalent is the Kadazan-Dusun harvest festival held in May. Again dancing and feasting are the major preoccupations, as well as buffalo races, games, and competitions.

SPIRITS ALL AROUND

With the introduction of the major world religions to Malaysia, and during the process of conversion, the local people retained and adapted their preexisting beliefs in spirits and deities—referred to in the technical literature as "animism," or "folk/popular religion." "Superstition" is a misleading term. Even devout believers in Islam or Christianity might still believe in the power and influence of the spirit world, and in any case, in Hinduism, Buddhism, and Chinese religion there is room for various kinds of benevolent ancestral and guardian spirits as well as those, like ghosts, that may bring harm to humans. Spiritual power may therefore reside in places, buildings, or objects, such as treasured heirlooms. Malaysians may still believe in the power of spells, love potions, charms, and amulets, and there are traditional practitioners who may be consulted in such matters as

illness, spiritual afflictions, augury, and fortunes. This is especially so among the indigenous populations of Malaysian Borneo, where harvest festivals are also intended to give thanks to the rice spirits and deities for a good harvest. You might even see a spirit house outside a Chinese dwelling or business premises.

chapter four

MEETING THE MALAYSIANS

There is more to conducting oneself in relations with others than being sensitive. If the visitor understands the cultural values underlying the forms of behavior explored in Chapter 2, adjustment should be easier. For those who are visiting Malaysia for a brief period as a tourist, or on a business trip, there are several useful tips on deportment, appropriate clothing, manners, and forms of address that will help to smooth casual encounters and interaction and assist you on more formal occasions. Chapters 6 and 8 provide more information on how to conduct yourself in superficial social exchanges, but for the expatriate who is living and working in Malaysia, and for the frequent visitor to the country, deeper friendships with Malaysians may develop over time.

FRIENDSHIP

Malaysians are generally hospitable, polite, and welcoming. However, it will usually take some time to make lasting friendships. Family ties are given priority in Malaysian society, and they provide a wide circle of support. Friends are therefore of rather less importance, though Malaysians tend to have a large number of casual acquaintances. As with family relationships, close and genuine friendships, like kinship ties, are based on mutual reciprocity and entail obligations to support and assist in times of need. They are also maintained by periodic gift giving. Keep in mind that religious

requirements affecting such things as diet and social relationships for Muslims may make it difficult for some non-Muslims to form very close bonds with them. It is perhaps easier to socialize with Chinese, Indian, and Dayak companions where a relaxing drink in a bar, club, or restaurant is permitted. Nevertheless, among all communities socializing with friends tends to take place outside the home, given the modest price of meals, the great range of cuisine available, and the fact that the warm evenings enable people to eat and entertain outdoors, in restaurants, hotels, cafés, and other eating places. For professional men from all ethnic groups such venues as the golf club on weekends are very popular, as is a shared meal or refreshments together after work.

GENERAL ETIQUETTE AND TOPICS TO AVOID

As we have already seen in general terms, the art and etiquette of social intercourse are considerably more important in Malaysia than in much of the West. The Western stress on individual rights and individualism contrasts with the greater social awareness and sense of community of Malaysians. Do not be fooled by things that look familiar to you and by the cosmopolitan and modern Malaysian who speaks fluent English and has been educated in the West. Deep-seated cultural differences remain. Also be careful of what you say about Malaysia and its history. Don't criticize the country's politics, economic system, or transportation system, or compare it unfavorably with your own. Privately Malaysians might agree with you, but they have been brought up in an independent, rapidly changing, and forward-looking country to which they have great loyalty, and they do not wish to be openly criticized or reminded of problems. Britons who think Malaysia was better under colonialism, and who wish to say so, should also think again! Overall, one should not be seen as interfering, especially in the political field.

Malaysia's ethnic relations have been a constant social and political preoccupation, and the foreign visitor should be wary about commenting on this element of present-day Malaysia. One particularly sensitive issue is that of intermarriage between ethnic groups, given that if a non-Muslim marries a Muslim then by law he or she will have to convert to Islam. Malaysians can sometimes be outspoken about such issues and about their society and their politics, but this does not give overseas visitors the right to do the same. The best advice is to be circumspect, but also to take a positive interest in local customs, cuisine, and language, and to accept hospitality. To break the ice with your Malaysian hosts, and especially the Malay community, a few words of the national language can help to build trust and closer relationships (see Chapter 9).

DEPORTMENT

The ways in which people move, conduct themselves, and use facial and bodily expressions are partly culturally determined and express either good manners or uncouth behavior. The general principles or values of consensus, harmony, and control are also interconnected with deportment and dress. In Malaysia it is not polite to point to or beckon someone with the index finger, or snap one's fingers at someone; nor should one point at animals. The accepted way is to point with the thumb, bending it slightly, with the fingers folded into the palm. A person can be summoned by holding the hand out, palm downward, and moving the fingers together toward the body. In short, one gestures or indicates discreetly with the hand and not in a pointed or direct way.

Don't behave in an impatient, annoyed, or aggressive manner. Don't stand in a swaggering way, with hands on hips. Casual touching in public between members of the opposite sex should also be avoided, as should any kind of kissing. Young people of the same sex sometimes walk together arm-in-arm. When walking out in a crowd, always keep your hands close to yourself, holding in your garments. Bumping into or brushing against people is not appreciated. These rules may not be rigorously observed when people are trying to get on to a crowded bus or train.

At formal gatherings in Malay and Indian houses you might find that men and women are separated, and you will be shown your appropriate place. Men will normally be seated in a front reception area, and the women in an inner room. When sitting, don't fold or cross your legs and point your foot at anyone, or show anyone the soles of your feet or shoes, which is considered very rude. It is best to keep both feet firmly on the ground. If you have to sit on the floor in Malay-style do not stick your legs straight out in front of you. Women especially should try to sit with both legs tucked to the side, left or right, with feet pointing away from guests or hidden under the hem of their skirt. Men may be permitted to sit cross-legged. Do not kneel or squat. Kneeling is used for an act of prayer, not on social occasions.

Finally, the head is considered a sacred or spiritual part of the body and should not be touched. A person's soul or a concentration of spiritual essence is thought to reside there and this may well derive from long-established folk beliefs that predated the introduction of

Buddhism and Islam to the region. In any case it is a very general belief in Southeast Asia found across a range of cultures and religions. You may think it helpful to brush an insect from someone's head, but don't do so. Don't pat a child's or a toddler's head or ruffle their hair. You shouldn't in any case touch or kiss someone else's child.

If you are visiting a Malaysian at home, slip your shoes off before entering, unless you are told otherwise. Even if your host does not insist it will be appreciated if you do remove your shoes.

DRESS

It is an obvious point, but worth emphasis. The foreign visitor should always attempt to dress conservatively—unless one is on the beach, or involved in a sporting activity or forest trekking. In major towns and tourist spots, flesh-revealing attire for women might not provoke much overt attention, but remember that Malaysia is a Muslim country, and especially in smaller places and rural areas, where one is likely to find many more Malay residents, dressing  immodestly is certainly not to be advised. A Muslim woman covers her head, arms, and legs. The foreign female visitor who exposes too much of the body, legs, midriff, shoulders, and back, or wears very tight-fitting clothes, will cause embarrassment to her hosts and, potentially, to herself.

In the humid tropics the general rule is to dress comfortably in light, usually loose-fitting, cotton clothing. For business meetings or any formal occasion or appointment, a lightweight dark or grey suit and a long-sleeved shirt and tie are appropriate for a man; rolled-up shirt sleeves should be avoided. For a woman, a smart blouse and knee-length skirt, a suit, or a long-sleeved dress are all suitable, though not with low necklines; trousers for women are increasingly seen, but may not always be appropriate, depending on the occasion. For attendance at special events such as weddings or a reception, the recommended dress is usually indicated on the invitation card.

For evening attire, a restaurant meal, a special occasion, or a wedding feast it might be specified that men can wear a cotton *batik* shirt. In Malaysia these are usually brightly colored and elaborately patterned. If you intend to stay for a while in the region or visit regularly then it might be worth purchasing a few shirts. They are very comfortable and versatile in tropical climes. Neither men nor women should wear all-black attire at Chinese New Year celebrations: black is associated with death. Nor should you wear all black at a Chinese wedding. Lighter suits for men and light-colored or patterned dresses and skirts for women are very appropriate.

GREETINGS

Because respect and honor are accorded to older people, you should greet and introduce yourself to them first. Do not stand back and expect them to come to you. This principle of good manners and deference to senior people is especially important in Malaysia. However, women are not normally given precedence in a sequence of introductions.

There are various traditional ways of greeting in Malaysia. A vigorous, pumping handshake, designed to demonstrate confidence and strength, is inappropriate, as is shoulder- or back-slapping, and arm- and elbow-grabbing. Embraces and kissing, however affectionate, informal, and friendly we might wish to be, are not advisable, and hand-kissing is certainly out. Some young Malaysian urbanites are now bucking the trend and have adopted Western modes of greeting, including the peck on the cheek and the embrace. Observe carefully what the local conventions are and follow others. Urbanized Malays, both men and women, may well shake hands with you, but this is usually quite a gentle handshake, more of a brief and light touch than a clasp. A woman may not offer her hand to be shaken, in which case a nod or a slight bow would be in order.

Malays might offer a traditional greeting—the *salam*. To respond properly you stretch out both hands and lightly touch both hands offered by your host; sometimes a fleeting touch of the fingertips is all that is required. You then withdraw your hands and bring them both to your heart or the lower part of your face. Using both hands shows respect or deference to someone who, for example, is senior or of higher status. Between equals the *salam* is sometimes performed with one hand, the right hand.

Chinese Malaysians will usually shake hands either between members of the same gender or between men and women, and they may incline their heads a little on first meeting. Indian men and women also commonly conform to the Western style of shaking hands. However, the Indian traditional greeting between men and women, which is also very common in Thailand, is for each person to put his or her palms together in a prayer position with the hands to the chest and a slightly bowed head. A little practice is all that is needed and once you get into the mode it is a most endearing and heartwarming greeting.

Malaysians also smile a lot, as do Southeast Asians in general. You should do so too, especially when you are greeting them and introducing yourself. But beware: smiles can mean different things. A wide grin is not appropriate.

FORMS OF ADDRESS
Personal Pronouns
Malaysians tend not to use the term "you," if possible, and prefer to use a title or personal name. They are always mindful of the importance of

establishing and maintaining culturally proper relations, which are directly expressed in forms of address. Once you know someone well, it may be appropriate to use their personal name, but using a title might still be preferred.

There are four words for "you" in Malay (*anda, saudara, kamu,* and *engkau*). The formal personal address for an outsider is usually *anda,* but a more informal usage, such as for small children or someone you know quite well, is *kamu* or *engkau.* Someone of similar age and status might also be addressed as *anda* or *saudara.*

The usual convention for addressing a senior person who requires respect is to call them *Puan* (lady) or *Tuan* (man). You may hear *Cik* for a young unmarried woman, though this is now considered rather old-fashioned, and *Encik* for a young man. *Puan* can also be used as a respectful form of address for unmarried women. *Tuan* is also a term of address that was used during the colonial period for a "white" or European man, while *Mem* was used for a woman.

Kinship

If there is a relationship that is neither too formal nor too informal, kinship terms may be used in addressing someone. For those in the senior generation *Datuk* (grandfather) and *Nenek* (grandmother), *Pakcik* (uncle) and *Makcik* (aunt) are appropriate, or *Abang* (elder brother) and *Kakak* (elder sister). For those of the younger generation *Adik* (younger brother or sister) is probably the most suitable term. But, given the pervasiveness of kinship ties and the Malaysian preoccupation with family you might find yourself addressed by such kinship terms as, "Uncle" or "Auntie," for example, in any circumstances. They are especially useful for people who are uncertain about your personal names, titles, or marital status.

Status and Hierarchy

The use of terms to refer to someone's status or occupation is most common (*Professor, Dokter, Guru* [Teacher], for example). A male schoolteacher is usually referred to as *Cikgu*, short for *Encik guru*. Be especially aware of a person's professional or honorific titles. Usually the most senior title takes precedence.

Malay society was traditionally strongly hierarchical, with a complex list of titles and statuses, and remains so to a large extent today; the immigrant communities have also been partially drawn into this system. Its complexities will provide you with hours of interest and fascination. It also embodies a whole host of requirements relating to appropriate behavior, etiquette, and forms of address, and it is therefore worth providing a little detail on this aspect of Malaysian culture.

Royal families, governors, and the federal authorities bestow honors and titles on deserving subjects. Royalty and the hereditary nobility also carry titles, sometimes an extended list of them. Royal status is indicated by such titles as *Sultan, Raja, Yang DiPertuan Besar,* and *Sultanah, Raja*

Perempuan, and *Tengku Ampuan*. The king, should you chance to be introduced to him, is, perhaps unexpectedly, referred to as His Majesty, though in Malay the honorific is a little more elaborate as *Duli Yang Maha Mulia Seri Paduka Baginda* (literally "The King who is made Supreme Ruler") or His Royal Highness (*Duli Yang Maha Mulia*). His consort

carries the same honorifics, though her title or rank is *Raja Permaisuri Agong*.

Other royal titles embrace crown princes, their consorts, other princes and princesses, titled royalty, and other members of the royal family. A good guide to royal status beyond the Sultan and Sultanah for princes and princesses is the use of the title *Tengku/Tunku* or *Raja*. Be aware that the formal mode of address to rulers, their consorts, and the crown princes is *Tuanku*; for consorts of crown princes *Ku Puan*, though for all others it is usually *Tengku/Tungku*.

There are variations between the different Malay states in titles or ranks and, because it comprised several subunits that were amalgamated, the state of Negeri Sembilan has its own titular system with the sultan styled *Yang Di Pertuan Besar* and his consort *Tunku Ampuan*, and there are four potential heirs apparent who are four senior members of the royal family each carrying their own title; other variations are seen in the designation of the heir apparent, which, in Johor, Kelantan, and Pahang is *Tengku/Tunku Mahkota*, in Kedah, Perak, Perlis, and Selangor, *Raja Muda*, and in Terengganu *Yang DiPertuan Muda*. The delightful subtleties of the Perak royal system and succession, where there are six designated princely titles and where the eldest son of a sultan does not automatically succeed to his father's position, defy simple explanation. The four states (Malacca, Penang, Sarawak, and Sabah) without a sultan have a governor styled *Yang DiPertua Negeri* and addressed as *Tuan Yang Terutama*, as are ambassadors and high commissioners. His consort carries her own title and name but has the honorific *Yang Amat Berbahagia*.

One of the most common conferred titles is *Datuk* (a title received from the federal government and state governors) and *Dato'* (a title conferred by royalty) for a man, and *Datin*, for a woman. If a woman does not hold a title in her own right she would be referred to as *Tok Puan* (wife of a *Dato'/Datuk*). There are also different grades of *Datuk*ship, including *Patinggi, Seri,* and *Paduka.* A *Datin Paduka* can be someone who has the title in her own right, but she could also be the wife of a *Datuk Paduka.* Higher titles such as *Tan Sri* (for men) and *Puan Sri* (for women), and *Tun* for a man and *Toh Puan* for the wife of a *Tun* should also be carefully noted and used. They are broadly equivalent to the English "Sir" and "Lady."

There are also honorifics appropriate for these various grades and for those appointed to senior government posts; for a *Tun* it is *Yang Amat Berbahagia* (The Most Fortunate), for a *Tan Sri* and *Datuk/Dato'* it is *Yang Berbahagia* (The Fortunate), for senior politicians the correct form of address is *Yang Amat Berhormat* (The Most Honorable) and *Yang Berhormat* (The Honorable).

There are also hereditary titles associated with Islam used among Muslim Malays, Indians, and Arabs, such as *Syed/Sayyid* and *Sharif* (male) and *Sharifah* (female), demonstrating links with the Prophet. A Muslim man who has been on the pilgrimage to Mecca (*haj*) is entitled to be addressed as *Haji* and a woman *Hajjah.* Other religious titles include *Imam* (leader of prayer at the mosque), *Kadhi* (registrar), *Mufti* (religious officer who also assists a judge), and *Ustaz* (a religious teacher).

PERSONAL AND FAMILY NAMES

Malay (and Muslim Indian) personal names are mainly derived from Arabic, but the same name may be spelled in a variety of ways, for example, Mohamad, Mohammad, Muhammad, and Mohamed. In Malay society it is a person's first name that should be used; for example, Rashid Abdullah or Rashid *bin* Abdullah is Rashid the son of Abdullah. He should be referred to and addressed as (Mr.) Rashid, or the equivalent in Malay, *Encik* Rashid, if a young man, and *Tuan* Rashid, if an older man.

A wife has her own name, and does not usually take her husband's name, but this is changing. Rahmah Talib, or in its full form Rahmah *binte/binti* Talib, is Rahmah the daughter of Talib. She could be referred to as *Puan* (Mrs.) Rahmah. However, things are becoming a little more confusing now in that she might be married to a man called Talib, and using his name. She would then be referred to as *Puan* Talib. Careful questioning is needed to establish the exact status of the name she is using.

Nothing in the labyrinth of Malay names and titles is straightforward, and a further complication is that some Malays are referred to as *Nik, Wan,* and *Megat,* or *Putri* for a woman. Some Malays will use these as family names and would be addressed as *Encik* Nik, and so on. Others, however, use them as titles that have some connection to royalty through the maternal line, in which case it would be inappropriate to use *Encik* and one should address them instead by their title.

Among Chinese the first name in the sequence is the family name, so Tan Chee Beng is Mr. Tan, and his personal names are Chee Beng; he is not Mr Beng. His wife can be called Mrs. Tan, but she has her own family name: Tai Ching Ling, for example. She could be referred to as Madam Tai, her first names being Ching Ling. Christian Chinese will commonly have a Christian name and Chinese personal and family names, and may be referred to, for example, as Michael Chen. Chinese names may also be rendered differently according to dialect so that a Mr. Goh can also be Wu or Ngu.

Most Indians do not have surnames as such. For example, a man referred to as B. Siva or Siva B. would be Mr. Siva, this being his personal name. The B. stands for his father's name, Bhaskaran. Officially he would be referred to as Siva s/o (son of) Bhaskaran. His wife Rajeswary could be referred to as Mrs. Siva, but she could also be called Madam Rajeswary. Some northern Indians do have family names, and use them, and there are Christian Indians who have Christian names. There are also those who under Portuguese influence in such places as Goa and Sri Lanka acquired such names as Da Cunha, De Alwis, Rozario, and Santa Maria. Sikh names are very distinctive in that the gender indicator for a male is Singh, used with a personal name such as Ranjit, thus Ranjit Singh. A female is indicated by the name Kaur, with a personal name such as Amarjit, thus Amarjit Kaur. A married woman may use her own names, or is sometimes referred to as Mrs. Singh, which is, in effect, a contradiction in terms.

Finally, many Dayak groups of East Malaysia are Christians, with Christian names, but they also have a personal Dayak name, which is often appended to the Christian name, for example Samuel Gana. Gana is not a surname, it is a given name. You may also find that Dayaks use a variant of the Malay form that is the personal name followed by the father's personal name, so Jayum Jawan is Jayum the son of Jawan. He should properly be referred to as Jayum, not Jawan. Sometimes the Malay word *anak*, meaning "child," is inserted, thus Jayum *anak* Jawan.

chapter five

THE MALAYSIANS AT HOME

HOUSING

There is a great variety of house styles in Malaysia, based on the different architectural designs and artistic traditions of the different ethnic groups, and also on regional variations in Malay and Dayak house forms. Traditionally, and still in

some rural areas today, Malays lived in houses raised on stilts above the ground and made of wood, thatch, palm leaves, and bark. Built leaving openings, and using natural materials that "breathe," these houses are designed to catch the breezes and allow a free flow of air. Stilted dwellings also provide protection against flood, extra storage space, and shelter for domestic animals. Even where the traditional design and layout remain, Malay housing is now more likely to comprise brick, concrete, tiles, glass, and plaster, though the raised brick house now provides convenient car-parking space below the living quarters.

For the Chinese the traditional two-story terraced urban shop house was the norm; it can still be seen in most towns and cities; business is conducted at the front of the premises, which opens on to a covered walkway connecting the separate houses, and the building then stretches back to contain the living quarters of the extended family on the ground and first floors. Indian merchants also usually occupied some of this shop house space in towns. In Malaysian Borneo, on the other hand, you can still see traditional Dayak longhouses, which in effect accommodate a whole village, the separate families living in terraced compartments raised on stilts, under one roof, and connected by a covered veranda which serves as the village street. Again, these longhouses are increasingly being built with modern materials, or are replaced with single family dwellings.

British colonial architecture often adapted traditional local designs, though houses were usually constructed from brick and plaster. Many grand detached colonial houses and mansions set in spacious grounds in secluded suburbs or in  landscaped estates on the edge of town and city centers have survived and are now the homes of wealthy Malaysians.

In towns and cities and in the rapidly expanding suburbs high-rise apartments and condominiums are found increasingly, as well as modern terraced and detached housing with gardens and undercover car parking. Some have been influenced by Western modernist architectural forms. However, certain of the design features of traditional Malay or Chinese housing may be retained, with distinctive roof forms, verandas, arches, and pillars. One also still sees in both urban and rural areas the dilapidated housing of the poor, reminiscent of the shanties and squatter settlements of the developing world. As Malaysia has modernized, makeshift housing is less evident now, and government authorities have also demolished most of the unsightly urban settlements and rehoused the residents in public and community housing schemes.

FAMILY LIFE

As we have seen, Malaysians are very family oriented. Children are cherished, and large families are common, though some couples practice family planning. A household, aside from mother, father, and children, will often contain a grandparent or two, and sometimes an unmarried aunt or uncle. A cousin might be staying in order to go to the local school or to work locally. With the demands of urban living, however, it seems that the extended family is gradually giving way to the nuclear family among younger, more socially and physically mobile Malaysians, but support from the wider family is still available and visits from other family members frequent. Although working mothers may hire domestic help for child care, family members are still usually preferred for this. Preschool children are cosseted, and always the center of adult attention and interest.

As children reach an age when they can be given greater responsibilities they are also frequently charged with looking after younger siblings and given household chores. They may also be called on to assist in the family business, particularly in the case of small Chinese and Indian concerns and Malay rural enterprises. This is all part of the set of social obligations between the junior and senior generations.

The emphasis that the Malaysian government has placed on education, especially since the launch of the New Economic Policy in 1970, has resulted in most families from all ethnic groups devoting time and resources to ensuring that their children receive support at school, college, and university. Middle-class Malaysians are preoccupied with the  importance of giving their children a good start in life, but these aspirations are also being strongly expressed among the urban and rural working classes. Parents in Malaysia generally want their children to do well, and to secure a well-paid job and a career path, and this has resulted in increasing movement of young people from the rural sector and agriculture to urban-based occupations.

No particular distinction is made between boys and girls, and increasing numbers of young women are now following courses in secondary and higher education. Islam is not a barrier to female education in Malaysia. Indeed in universities women outnumber men two to one. The federal government provides free education at both primary and secondary levels; primary education is compulsory from the age of six and older family members willingly provide support for younger relatives to enable them to complete their studies successfully. The medium of instruction is Bahasa Malaysia, but the government is gradually reintroducing English into the curriculum, especially in science teaching. There is a good range of private and international schools for expatriate children, but most go up only to primary level, and these tend to be oversubscribed. Therefore it is important to get your child's name on the list and to reserve a place.

From 2003 the Malaysian government introduced a National Service Program for young men and women from all ethnic groups who have turned seventeen years of age. As a result of a shortage of resources, trainers, and training camps, the scheme does not embrace all those young people of the appropriate age. Instead, 20 percent of those eligible are chosen randomly. In 2003 it was 85,000 conscripts out of a total of 450,000 citizens born in 1986; and 100,000 youths were conscripted in 2007. Training is relatively short and lasts for three months. Exemptions are, of course, granted for those with special personal circumstances.

For all young Malaysians marriage is a valued institution. Young people living together out of wedlock are frowned upon. However, with the expansion of higher education and training for men and women there is an increasing tendency toward later marriage and childbearing. A successful marriage in the eyes of the family is when children are born. Childless couples usually seek to adopt, and in fact often adopt a child from close relatives. A young married couple does not necessarily establish an independent household right away, and may live with the parents of either husband or wife for a considerable period.

Aging or widowed parents might move into the household of a married son or daughter to ensure that they are looked after in their remaining years, and they help with children and household tasks in return for this support.

DAILY ROUTINE

For most Malaysians the day starts early, when it is still relatively cool. Many schools commence at 8:00 a.m., and government offices, commercial, and business premises also open early, at 8:00 to 8:30 a.m.; they shut for lunch at some time between 12 noon and 2:00 p.m., and then go on until 4:30 p.m., Mondays to Fridays. Offices are usually closed on Saturdays. Private companies are usually open between 9:00 a.m. and 5:00 or 6:00 p.m., and are open for a half day on Saturdays between 9:00 a.m. and 1:00 p.m. On Friday there is also some variation in hours when Muslims go to the mosque for prayers. Offices are usually shut by 11:30 a.m. or noon, and staff return to work at 2:30 or 2:45 p.m., and then go on to 4:15 p.m. In Terengganu, Kelantan, and Kedah the Muslim weekly calendar is followed in government offices, banks, and some retail outlets; they close on Friday and open on Sunday, with Thursday as a half day. Banks are usually open from 10:00 a.m. to 3:00 p.m. For shopping, store hours are very generous; department stores and shopping malls usually open from 10:00 a.m. to 10:00 p.m., though some smaller shops may open earlier and close by 7:00 p.m.

Therefore, the Malaysian family usually rises between 6:00 and 7:00 a.m. for breakfast at home.

An alternative is to have breakfast on the way to work, in a coffee shop or at one of the roadside stalls, which are ready for business very early. In the busy urban conglomerations with all the problems of traffic jams, an early start is also a means to beat the traffic and avoid some delays. By 7:00 or 7:30 a.m. roads are already crowded;

local fruit and vegetable, meat, and fish markets and stalls are open; women, and sometimes men, are taking their children to school, and looking for fresh food for the family's meals.

In rural areas people's lives are organized around the demands of the agricultural cycle and the climate. To avoid too much exposure to the heat of the day agricultural and estate workers start even earlier, at about 6:00 a.m., with several short breaks during the morning, until lunchtime. They may also take a longer break during the early afternoon, and then work later in the afternoon and early evening when it is cooler.

With the expansion of the Malaysian economy many more women now work outside the home, though the numerous small family retail businesses, particularly Chinese shops, require husbands, wives, and children after school hours to be available on the premises.

Most offices, modern shops, and cars are equipped with air-conditioning ("air-con"), so people are in an artificially cool environment for most of the day. For those unused to working in hot, humid climes this provides a comfortable environment that prevents you from becoming sleepy later in the day. You can still also see traditional ceiling fans, and other places will have free-standing electric fans.

Malaysians often take a brief mid-morning break, with a longer break at lunchtime. Most premises with Muslim employees will provide prayer rooms for the noon and mid-afternoon prayer times. The midday break in Malaysia is usually a leisurely affair, lasting for about one to one-and-a-half hours. Workers often bring their own packed lunch, or buy something from a local shop or stall and take their break on the premises, or go to a cafeteria or other public space to relax and chat. Given the wide availability of cheap, wholesome food with basic dishes of rice or noodles, soup, curried or stir-fried meat, or fish and vegetables, many people pop into their local favorite coffee shop, restaurant, or food court for a hot meal with coffee or tea.

A Bit Too Cool!

On occasion, the Malaysians' enthusiasm for "air-con" gets the better of them; some are so used to working in a bracing atmosphere that they turn the temperature down even further. While working in an office or sitting in a restaurant one sometimes finds oneself reaching for one's jacket as goose bumps begin to appear!

By mid-afternoon the heat and humidity outside can be quite debilitating. The working day usually finishes at about 4:00 p.m. for those in the public sector. Private establishments often go on until 5:00 p.m., and retail outlets and eating places much longer. Some workers go off with colleagues and friends for a drink or snack, but usually people are at home by about 7:00 p.m. for their evening meal and a relaxing evening, watching television, reading, or playing games with the children. In Kuala Lumpur and the Klang Valley traveling in the "rush hour" from 4:00 through 7:00 p.m. should be avoided if possible.

During the working week the early morning start requires most people to go to bed reasonably early. On occasion a family may go out to eat in the week, but this is more likely on weekends.

EXPATRIATE LIVING

Of course some foreign business and commercial people, and indeed others, such as overseas government contract workers, teachers, and lecturers, may be posted longer term to Malaysia. Most expatriates live in the major cities and towns, particularly Kuala Lumpur, Klang, Penang, Johor Bahru, Kuching, and Kota Kinabalu. There are few, if any, difficulties in these locations. The company or employer will usually provide or help to find accommodation, and may give a housing allowance. Rented accommodation is normally of a good standard, with air-conditioning (a must), well-appointed kitchens, modern bathrooms with shower, and fully furnished. It will probably be an apartment in a new high-rise development or a semidetached or detached house in a conveniently located and well-tended suburban estate. Many modern apartment complexes have a shared leisure area with a swimming pool.

You will also invariably share your apartment or house, however modern, with teeming insect

life. Sprays and slow-burning repellents keep
much of this at bay. Ants tend to get everywhere,
but try to keep cockroaches out of the kitchen.
Don't be alarmed when small lizards (geckos)
scamper over your floors, walls, and ceilings.

Household Help

Domestic help is easily available and reasonably
priced. You may inherit a domestic helper from
the previous occupant, or you can ask friends and
colleagues. Agencies, however, are now the main
method of recruitment, and wages and conditions
of service are set down in advance. Depending on
your status, salary, and the size of your house and
garden, you may want to engage more than one
domestic helper, a gardener, and a driver.

You should use written references as well as
word of mouth to check someone out, and
interview them, but it can be a bit hit-and-miss.
Check the passport and identity card, and
establish the religion and any requirements that
this entails, of your prospective employee. You
will be looking for honesty, discretion, experience,
and conscientiousness. Most household help
comprises migrant workers from the Philippines
(who usually speak at least some English) and
Indonesia (who usually don't, unless they have
already worked for an English-speaking family);
sometimes these are unmarried girls, who often
need close supervision and training, sometimes
married women with children whom they left
back home. Migrant workers will usually live in,

and most accommodation will have rooms for them. If you are employing a local maid, find out all you can about her background and personal circumstances; again, depending on where her home area is she may need to live in; those who live close by usually come in daily when required.

From the outset you must be clear about what you expect of your household helper, and what free time she is allocated. A domestic servant or maid (*amah*) usually helps with household shopping (but if you prefer to shop for yourself there are numerous supermarkets, specialty shops, and fruit and vegetable markets and stalls). You may want her to cook, or at least prepare the food. In this climate, laundry and ironing are major tasks for which domestic help is essential. You may also need help with child care. Training and supervision will be necessary until you are satisfied that your helper has ample experience.

Keeping in mind the Malaysian cultural context, you will get the best out of your domestic helpers if you treat them fairly, politely, and with consideration rather than barking direct orders at them and scolding them for doing something of which you do not approve.

If you are posted to Malaysia, the simple and obvious advice is to seek help and information from others with experience of expatriate life there. Also, look at the Web sites and blogs about expatriate living—they make fascinating reading.

chapter six

TIME OUT

LEISURE

With their large number of relatives around them, on almost immediate call, Malaysians spend most of their spare time with, and have most of their entertainment provided by, the family. There always seems to be a birth, wedding, funeral, or other rite of passage to attend, or some other special event—securing an educational qualification, promotion at work, or settling into a new home—to celebrate. These, in addition to the weekly and calendrical round of community religious events, ceremonies, and festivals, absorb much leisure interest and time.

As we have seen, socializing with friends and visitors usually takes place outside the home. The wealthy, with spacious living quarters, may entertain at home, but for most Malays, who already have a houseful of people, it is much more convenient to meet with friends, acquaintances, and foreign visitors for dinner in a nearby restaurant.

The emphasis on family-oriented activities means that the Western notion of leisure, based much more on packaged entertainment, is rather less important in Malaysia. However, with increasing affluence and the emergence of a substantial middle class, there is an increasing demand for commercially organized entertainments, such as theater, concerts, and film. Affluent Malaysians, with four weeks' vacation a year, as well as weekends and public holidays, are also traveling more; domestic tourism is booming, with sightseeing, shopping, and relaxation at beach resorts or national parks, forest reserves, and wildlife sanctuaries. Weekend breaks to vacation resorts are very popular, and Malaysian tourists are now seeking out other destinations. Singapore, Thailand, and Indonesia are especially attractive. There is also still interest in traditional Asian art and performance, such  as Chinese opera, Malay shadow puppets, martial arts, Qu'ran recitals, and dance routines such as *joget*, which are regularly shown on television.

Malaysians have a wide range of leisure activities available to them, aside from watching television, surfing the Internet, and playing computer games. Eating out, shopping, and sports seem to be paramount, and you will find crowds in restaurants and other eating places, in malls and open-air markets, and in sports clubs and complexes. If there is any national sport that commands an inordinate amount of attention, aside from badminton and table tennis, in which Malaysians excel, it is watching English premiership football and, of course, playing football. There are quite vigorous state and local level football leagues. Traditionally Malaysians have not been particularly attracted to picnics at beauty spots or beaches, or trekking through jungles and uplands, though this is changing.

In cities and towns, and especially in Kuala Lumpur and Penang, there is a nightlife, bar, and

club culture, and often hotels with a cabaret act, usually with a resident Filipino band. It is primarily the Chinese and some of the Indian community that take advantage of these. The main gambling resort in the Genting Highlands is frequented by local Chinese, Singaporeans, and tourists from other parts of Asia and beyond. It does not attract the Malay community.

THE FOREIGN COMMUNITY

There is much for the expatriate and the short-term visitor to Malaysia to do, quite apart from sightseeing. There are various national associations with their own club facilities, mainly based in Kuala Lumpur, though there are also some in Penang—American, British, German, Italian, French, and Japanese. They provide a focus for social activities, offer advice and support in looking for accommodation, schools, and domestic help, and produce their own newsletters and bulletins. There are also numerous clubs that you can join—golf, tennis, swimming, football, cricket, tennis, squash, fitness, bridge—the choice is wide. The hot, sunny weather means that outdoor sports can be played all year-round, though heat and humidity can take their toll on the fair-skinned foreigner who is not used to vigorous exercise in such an environment. To discuss business affairs the golf club is a must, and to get access to a swimming pool, in the absence of good municipal facilities, joining a club is essential. Sports, leisure, and fitness clubs are also ideal places to socialize with local people.

Much of the social service provision that is taken for granted in the West is undertaken by voluntary organizations and charities in Malaysia. Partners of those who have a work contract in Malaysia can find plenty to do in the areas of fund-raising, clerical support, teaching, training, working with deprived children and the disabled, and English-language teaching. Facilities for the pursuit of special interests are also numerous, with clubs and associations for music, opera, amateur dramatics, dance, art, needlework, and local history, among many others.

EATING OUT AND TABLE MANNERS

Eating is a major preoccupation in Malaysia, and you may need to watch your weight! It is worth bearing in mind that the climate is not conducive to vigorous and sustained outdoor walking and exercise, or, for some, even a more measured stroll, unless you are in air-conditioned facilities, so burning off calories may not be an easy option. Or you could just forget about fitness and weight and be prepared to feast on a wonderful range of cuisines. A common greeting or inquiry in Malay is *Sudah makan?* (Have you eaten?). Malaysians love the company, entertainment, and warmth that go with sharing a meal, and they will be especially pleased if they see that you enjoy their food and hospitality. The evening meal usually starts at about 7:00 or 7:30 p.m.

For the business visitor, sharing food with potential partners is a very important element in building a relationship. Expect an invitation, or several, to a good restaurant. Working breakfasts and lunches are increasingly common. The Chinese are particularly keen on business entertaining. But there is another dimension to eating to remember: food and cooking are part of culture, and, as we know, they give expression to religious differences. Food is therefore subject to various cultural requirements and restrictions.

Coffee Shops and Food Stalls

A common sight is the coffee shop (*kedai kopi*), where breakfast is often taken before the start of the working day and where friends and colleagues can catch up on news and prepare for the day. There is nothing more pleasurable than a breakfast of freshly cooked noodles and seafood with a large mug of tea or coffee.

The Perfect Breakfast

One of my most treasured experiences is the early-morning Malay meal of *nasi lemak*, which I used to have with a friend on the outskirts of the city of Ipoh in Perak, sitting in the cool of the morning under a palm tree: rice garnished with spicy curried sauce (sometimes containing small pieces of beef, chicken, lamb, or squid), little dried and salted fish, peanuts, and cucumber. Another favorite was prawn soup with noodles (*mee udang*). My e-mails to my friend usually end "I'm missing breakfast under the tree."

Just as ubiquitous is the food stall. These are located in the coffee shops, food hawker centers, and covered market areas, as well as on the open streets. They usually offer light snack meals: noodles, soups, rice porridge, dumplings, deep-fried cakes with or without meat, curries, Indian  breads, and pancakes. Each stall specializes in a particular dish or set of dishes, with a separate stall (and fridge) serving drinks—tea and coffee in all their wonderful varieties, bottled drinks, and, for later in the day, beer (in the non-Muslim shops). You can also get rather more ample meals at lunchtime, and many of the food centers with their varieties of stalls are popular family attractions in the evenings. Generally these stalls are clean, with good standards of hygiene, and excellent value. But for the first-time visitor it is sensible to be careful and to order cooked food rather than salads, and either hot or bottled drinks.

Chinese Food
It goes without saying that in a Chinese restaurant it is a useful skill to be able to use chopsticks, and at a Chinese banquet it is difficult to avoid this. Chinese food definitely tastes better eaten from chopsticks. But it is not absolutely essential, and you can usually reach for the spoon and fork, utensils that you would normally use in Malay and Indian restaurants. Remember that with chopsticks the bottom stick remains fixed and the top one is mobile and has all the hard work to do. Don't try to pierce food with a chopstick, and try not to get your sticks crossed. When you pause between courses, or have finished eating, the ends of the chopsticks that go in the mouth should always be placed away from you, either on a small stand or holder provided, or on your side plate. It is acceptable to bring the rice bowl occasionally from the table to your mouth and, using your chopsticks, gently push or slide the rice into your mouth.

The Chinese soup spoon, usually of porcelain, is very versatile and can be used for scooping up virtually anything. If you have something to dispose of (bones, gristle, or something that you have placed in your mouth but find difficult to swallow) a side plate is normally available for the purpose. If you are not provided with one, then politely ask for one, or place the unwanted items on the rim of your main plate.

You will also usually have a small dish, or two dishes, for vinegar or soya and, if you wish, a mix of freshly chopped chilies. You dip pieces of meat and any other morsels into this for additional flavoring. Beware the small green and red chilies; they can be fiery. The larger green ones are milder, and delicious in vinegar. If you want more, ask for it. Your host will be delighted that you have an appetite and are enjoying the food, but at a banquet you can help yourself in any case.

Sometimes rice is served with the main dishes, or it may be the penultimate dish, followed by fresh fruit or other desserts, with ample supplies of Chinese tea, and beer if you wish. Expensive cognac or whiskey appear on special occasions.

Sometimes your host will place choice morsels of food on your plate at a first serving. This is a thoughtful gesture, so accept and eat them graciously. Refusing food in Malaysia has to be handled sensitively and diplomatically, and it is always best to try a little. Then, if you must, leave it on your side plate. Do not refuse outright.

Pace Yourself

A word of warning; unless you have a gargantuan appetite do not take too much food in the early courses of a Chinese banquet. Each course is delivered on a circular turntable and the diners sit around a circular table. You may be served with a first helping, and then help yourself from the turntable. There may be five courses for a modest meal, seven for something a little more special, and nine if very special. It is sometimes difficult to anticipate how many courses will be arriving.

Traditional Malay Food

In a traditional Malay or southern Indian setting you might be invited to eat with your fingers, or to be more precise the fingers of your right hand (the left hand for Muslims and Hindus is used for personal hygiene). Many Malaysians are happy to use either utensils or fingers: for a relaxing lunch at an everyday restaurant, and especially when rice with curry is served, they prefer to use their fingers, but at an evening meal in a restaurant often use a spoon and fork. Rice in particular is eaten with a spoon, not a fork. With Indian hosts you might not only be invited to take food with your fingers but also eat from a banana leaf (which serves as a plate, and is not part of the meal).

You will invariably be supplied with a bowl of water or a water vessel (*kendi*) to wash or rinse your right hand. Tissues are usually provided as well, but in some restaurants you simply go to the nearest cold-water faucet and rinse your hands. Of course you can carry your own tissues. Drinking glasses are placed to the left because you will make quite a mess if you try to eat and drink with your right hand.

With Malay and Indian hosts you are unlikely to be served anything stronger than tea, coffee, or light fruit drinks, though some Indian hosts may offer alcohol. You must take note of Muslim dietary requirements, not only the absence of alcohol, but also the prohibition against eating pork. Meat that can be eaten must be positively designated as *halal* (slaughtered in the manner prescribed by Muslim law). You will see signs in supermarkets, shops, and food outlets indicating whether the meat there is *halal*. It is unlikely that Muslims will go to Chinese restaurants if pork is served there and if the meat is not *halal*, though some Chinese restaurants serve food appropriate for Muslims and usually display large notices to inform their customers that they do so.

In mixed company it may become slightly trickier. Hindus and Sikhs do not eat beef. In these situations chicken or lamb dishes are often safe bets, but some Indians are fully vegetarian and others are vegetarians who will take milk products. This is now less of an issue for Western diners, with the increasing number who prefer a vegetarian lifestyle, and in any case there are many superb vegetarian restaurants in Malaysia.

Malay food is generally hotter or spicier than Chinese food, and closer to the Indian style, with a variety of curried and spiced dishes. For the foreign visitor accustomed to Indian curries, eating Malay food is not a problem. Common additions are fermented prawn paste, or *belachan*, turmeric, chili, cloves, anise, pepper, cumin, caraway, and fenugreek. Coconut milk is used copiously. If you are invited to eat out your host will order a variety of dishes with different degrees of "heat," but will usually ask if you have favorite dishes and whether or not you eat spicy food. For someone who finds chili a problem, there are many mildly spiced and delicious meat, fish, and vegetable dishes to try. Do not assume that only one dish is for you; the idea is to take a little from a variety of dishes on offer.

If you are a guest, you would not be expected to pay, or to share the cost. The host takes care of the bill. You can reciprocate at some later date, but you should seek advice on where to take your guests, and ensure that you know what their religion is and the food permitted and forbidden to them. You might ask them to indicate their favorite restaurant before booking.

Remember that in Ramadan (Puasa), the Muslim fasting month, you would only be invited to a meal after sunset, and a business visitor should not expect to hold a meeting over lunch. At this time business meetings are best held in the morning, and office hours are usually adjusted; there is a shorter lunch break and earlier closing hours. It is not appropriate to eat or drink in the presence of someone who is fasting. In the few hours of early morning and evening, women are busy preparing food, and it is best not to call casually at a Muslim home during this time.

TIPPING

Many restaurants and hotels, especially if they take credit cards, add a 10 percent service charge to the bill, along with a 5 percent government tax. You can add something further if you have had really good service. If a service charge is not included, a 10 percent tip might be given. Loose change may be given to taxi and trishaw drivers, or the fare rounded up; hotel porters and other bag carriers may be given a few Malaysian dollars.

A Rich and Varied Cuisine

If you like experimenting with food, you will have hours of enjoyment in Malaysia—and perhaps more hours of post-visit dieting. Many foreign visitors are already familiar with Malay *sate/satay* (skewered grilled meat with a dip of curried peanut sauce, and side relishes of cucumber and onion). The Chinese takeout version in Britain is often a

curious adaptation of this dish. Then there is the favorite local breakfast dish of *nasi lemak* (see page 109), and the popular evening dish *rendang* (usually beef long simmered in spices, chili, and coconut milk until relatively dry).

Chinese cuisine is now known the world over, and there are superb restaurants in Malaysia with excellent standards. For a lighter meal there are the many different varieties of noodles (*mee*) with soup, or Chinese snacks (*dim sum*)—dumplings, rolls, puffs filled with meat, prawns, and fish, and spicy spare ribs. For the gourmet shark's fin, turtle eggs (though there are increasing restrictions on these), sea cucumber, and bird's nests are worth a taste. Try also *Nonya*-style (or *Nyonya-Baba*) cooking, characteristic of the long-settled Chinese communities of Penang and Malacca, which provides a delightful blend of Chinese and Malay cuisine, and has produced the delicious thick noodle soup cooked with coconut milk (*laksa*), either served in curried form or with sour fish. Indian griddle cakes or pancakes (generally called *roti*) have to be tried; they come in all shapes, sizes, and textures, with different sauces. A favorite is *roti chanai*, a thin bread with pea or lentil curry sauce, washed down with "pulled tea" (*teh tarik*), a frothy, milky tea. For its enthusiasts this combination makes an excellent breakfast.

Not For the Fainthearted

The truly adventurous might be tempted by a Chinese menu that I recently sampled. Among the delights on offer—and I list them as they were written—were: potato and frog with rice, spice frog, steamed frog rice with lotus, frog rice with bamboo or wood cup, salt and pepper duck beak, pearl octopus, pig bowel with rice, hot pepper duck gizzard. You might also like to try a light snake soup, with an aperitif of snake gall and blood mixed with liquor.

Dining Etiquette

Most Malaysians are quite flexible and relaxed about table manners. The major concerns are the food and the company. However, apart from the tips given above, there are some other aspects of Asian-style eating that deserve a brief mention.

Soup and other liquids can be slurped: noisy eating is fine with Malaysians. If you want to remove an indigestible item of food from your mouth during the meal, do so with chopsticks, spoon, or fingers. It is unlikely that anyone will mind. Don't be offended if someone burps at the end of the meal; it is not considered rude, but is a clear indication that the food has gone down well and been appreciated.

You may often see, especially in a Chinese restaurant, where there is no tablecloth and a surface that can be easily wiped over, that food remnants are simply placed on the table beside the plate. After a wonderful meal including a medley of chili crab, steamed fish in ginger and spring onion, shellfish with garlic, and fried chicken, the table will look like a battlefield, with empty shells, claws, fish and chicken bones, and other scraps scattered all around. All the signs of an excellent meal, greatly appreciated. You may well find that cats are in attendance, some rather scrawny and unkempt, wandering under tables and chairs and scavenging for leftovers.

Toothpicks are ubiquitous, and it seems quite natural to use them, even if you do not do so at home. You should place your other hand over your mouth to hide what you are doing.

It is wise to carry some lavatory paper with you. While some restrooms are clean and well equipped, others are not.

SHOPPING FOR PLEASURE

Malaysia is a shopper's paradise. It is the ideal place to shop for a large range of consumer goods, at least in the main towns and cities of the peninsula. Sarawak and Sabah tend to be more expensive, but even so the advantageous exchange rates with US dollars and sterling mean that local prices are very attractive.

If you are a lazy shopper for handicrafts you can go to the standard government craft centers, where you will find a good range —but at tourist prices. If you like to shop around, there are many small shops selling locally produced items, although you might have to bargain. Even so, prices are generally much more reasonable. Local goods to look out for are batiks, Selangor pewter, silver filigree jewelry,

Malay silver and gold threaded woven textiles, woven cloths from Sarawak, and a range of indigenous crafts from Malaysian Borneo, including rattan baskets, wood carvings, and

beadwork. Chinatowns can supply locally woven cloth, baskets, containers, and hats, and Indian shops are good for textiles in any material, including cotton and silk. There are also increasing amounts of highly priced "antique" crafted items on sale. Some of these might be genuine, but most of them are fakes, with special techniques applied to give the appearance of age.

In Kuala Lumpur the very touristy market in Chinatown at Petaling Street is worth a visit, as is the equally touristy and very colorful covered Central Market. There are the smarter shopping malls at KL City Center (Suria KLCC), and those who want a much wider choice and price range, with bargaining, should visit Bukit Bintang Plaza and the adjoining Sungei Wang Plaza in the main hotel area. For a mind-blowing shopping experience try the Megamall at Mid Valley City, Lingaran Syed Putra. These malls are usually open from 10:00 a.m. until 10:00 p.m. Duty-free shopping beyond airports requires a longer-distance trip to Langkawi or Labuan.

Bargaining

At markets and in local shops, bargaining is essential and expected. And in shopping malls, although prices are marked on commodities, don't assume they are fixed. If you don't like the cut and thrust of bargaining, or find it too exhausting, you can simply ask for a discount. You will probably be given a modest reduction.

Start by offering half the price quoted. Remain good-humored and polite, and keep smiling: unpleasantness and aggression will not produce the desired result, but calm persistence will. However, even when you have the satisfaction of tirelessly beating down the salesperson, in between periodically trying to edge out of the shop and then succumbing to the request to reengage in the bargaining encounter, you know, deep down, that as a foreign visitor or tourist you are still probably paying more than a local customer.

SIGHTSEEING

There are many things to see in Malaysia, in both urban and rural settings: town markets, especially those held in the evenings, are a must; food hawker centers; places of worship; Chinese shop houses; colonial architecture; and museums. As a general rule, shoes should be removed when you enter temples and mosques, though this is not usually necessary in Chinese temples. Just follow what local people do. You may also buy incense sticks in the temple and light them, holding them in both hands and gently waving them in front of you while you pray or make a wish. When entering a mosque, remember the rules of decorum (see pages 55–6).

The main tourist centers, aside from Kuala Lumpur, are Penang (with the island resort of Langkawi not far from Penang) and Malacca, and in Malaysian Borneo Kuching (and adjoining resorts such as Santubong and the Sarawak Cultural Village near the Damai Beach resort) and Kota Kinabalu (with the adjoining hotel and beach area of Tanjung Aru).

Penang is the vacation island that has everything—a historic town center on the eastern side of the island packed with old shop houses, temples, churches, mosques, and colonial buildings, beautiful beaches and resorts in the north, and quieter Malay villages, rural areas, and plantations in the west. Those who want to visit museums, historic buildings, mosques, temples, colonial architecture and shops will obviously go to the main towns and cities. If you have time, however, it is worth going off the beaten path to soak up the local flavor.

In rural areas picturesque villages, tropical beaches, and coastal scenery, dramatic, forest-covered interior uplands, and the variations in natural landscapes and glimpses of wild life in national parks provide enduring images and visual experiences. Good beaches are abundant on the east coast of the peninsula and some of the idyllic offshore islands. There has been a very large increase in ecotourism in recent years, with such associated activities as diving, bird- and animal-watching, and mountain climbing. The following are just a few of the places to see to experience the natural landscapes of Malaysia:

- **The Cameron Highlands**, a center for the cultivation of Malaysia's market garden products, tropical and temperate, and examples of British colonial architecture in the old hill station areas.
- **Taman Negara**, peninsular Malaysia's first national park, originally named King George V Park in 1939, and containing one of the earth's oldest undisturbed rain forests with a large range of flora and fauna and communities of *orang asli*.
- **Mount Kinabalu**, a national park with the highest mountain in Southeast Asia and dramatic views; it's a relatively easy climb to the top; but it's safest to go with a guide. The park is home to the *Rafflesia*, the largest flower in the world.
- **Endau-Rompin National Park**, with a vast area of lowland tropical rain forest and Malayan tigers and elephants, and rhinoceros.
- **Pulau Tioman**, off the east coast of peninsular Malaysia, and Langkawi, tropical islands with wonderful beaches.
- **Batu Cave**, a sacred Hindu shrine near Kuala Lumpur, with 272 steps up to the cave, and the focus of the Hindu ceremony of Thaipusam.

- **Genting Highlands**, picturesque uplands with casinos.
- **Niah Caves**, dramatic limestone caves in a national park consisting of peat swamp and dense dipterocarp forest. It provides evidence of early man in Southeast Asia from about 40,000 years ago in the excavated burial areas of the west mouth of Niah Great Cave. The complex also contains the "Painted Cave" with paintings and burial remains from some 2,000 years ago.
- **Mulu Caves**, reputedly containing the world's largest cave, the Sarawak Chamber, passageways, and limestone pinnacles, set in a well-preserved rain forest and national park.
- **Semenggoh**, a sanctuary for *orang utans* not far from Kuching in Sarawak.
- **Bako**, the oldest Sarawak park, has dramatic coastal scenery of steep cliffs, sea arches and stacks, and sandy bays. Home to macaques,  silver leaf monkeys, proboscis monkeys, monitor lizards, mouse deer, and wild boar.

This list is a very modest taste of what is on offer; you will need much more than a two-week vacation to see and experience all the fascinating and beautiful sights of Malaysia.

chapter seven

TRAVEL, HEALTH, & SAFETY

The Malaysian transportation infrastructure is of a reasonably high standard, but there are some matters to keep in mind when you are planning your trips. Variations in climate can affect travel at certain times of the year. Although Malaysia has a relatively even rainfall throughout the year, the northeast monsoon can be especially severe on the east coast of the peninsula from October and November through to January and February, and along the northeast coasts of Borneo from October to April in Sarawak and to February in Sabah. Heavy rains, high winds, and flooding can occur in exposed regions. Some peninsular east coast facilities might close down for a time during the monsoon period, and boat services are sometimes disrupted.

Malaysia is a relatively large country, and is divided into two parts separated by the South China Sea. The only sensible way to move between the western and eastern parts of Malaysia is by air (unless you happen to be on a cruise). The era of the Straits Steamship Company, when one could sail majestically across the South China Sea from Singapore to Kuching in three days, is pretty much over. And you cannot always count on the main line rail service that connects Singapore via Kuala Lumpur to Penang. If you wish to see as much of the country as possible within a limited amount of time, you will probably decide to take domestic flights, particularly if you are on a two- or three- resort vacation that includes both the Peninsula and Malaysian Borneo.

If you want to visit national parks, good beaches, and some of the remoter parts of interior Sarawak and Sabah, allow for possible delays on roads and rivers. Although the main roads are good, once you get on to minor roads you will need to allow plenty of time. Delays can be caused by weather conditions as well, and river levels are notoriously changeable both in and out of the monsoon season.

Roads can easily be inundated or washed away if they are not, or are only partially, surfaced.

Maps in Malaysia are improving in quality. Street maps of the main towns and cities, particularly Kuala Lumpur, Penang, Malacca, Johor Bahru, Kuching, and Kota Kinabalu are serviceable, but sometimes not sufficiently detailed. These can be obtained from most hotel reception desks and tourist information offices. For smaller places you sometimes have to take your chance and follow your nose. The best road maps are produced by foreign publishers.

If you want to get out and about, and it is not part of your overall vacation package, drop into a reputable travel agent or go to the appropriate office or desk in your hotel and see what they can do for you. They may also be able to pick up good discounted deals on hotel or other accommodation and some even better deals if it is out of season. Of course, it is easiest if you have your transportation requirements (flight, bus, boat, or car with a driver) built into the package rather than having to organize your own method of travel.

WALKING

For the foreign visitor unused to a humid tropical climate it is not advisable to dash around the towns and countryside on foot, or certainly not until you are fully acclimatized. Depending on your state of physical health you might find that short walks in town for sightseeing and shopping are all that you can manage, interspersed with moments of respite in an air-conditioned mall, in a taxi, or on a bus. Use sidewalks, underpasses, and overpasses; some Malaysian drivers can be a bit unpredictable. Don't expect high standards of sidewalk maintenance.

Plan your itineraries carefully. Allow plenty of time, and make sure you can find a taxi or bus if you need to get out of the sun and off your feet. For the fair-skinned visitor, sunblock, hat, and umbrella are useful; an umbrella protects against the sun and the sudden heavy tropical downpour. For a woman, covering the shoulders and arms when walking in town is both a way of ensuring one's modesty and protecting against sunburn.

Mind Your Step

When walking in Kuala Lumpur, Ipoh, Penang, Kota Kinabalu, and Kuching, I sometimes wonder how anyone who is disabled or who has difficulty walking can negotiate the street hazards. There are often broken sidewalks, missing drain and sewer covers, half-finished road works, and other obstacles. These are complicated by the need for high sidewalks and storm drains to cope with tropical downpours.

After or during heavy rain there are the added problems of flooding, standing water, and slippery walkways. Recently, wearing what I thought were sensible shoes (but which obviously did not have nonslip soles), I crashed down a flight of steps outside a Kuala Lumpur shopping mall after heavy rainfall. The top step, smooth and sloping slightly downward, was treacherous.

Despite the hazards of walking it is far more sensible than going on a bicycle (motorized or otherwise), unless you are very adventurous, fearless in traffic, extremely fit, and fully protected against the sun. If you are a bike enthusiast then you could hop into a rickshaw. They are gradually disappearing from the Malaysian streets, but still numerous in such places as George Town in Penang. They provide a leisurely way of seeing street life in the cool of the early evening.

TAXIS

You are spoiled for choice. In urban areas taxis are a good bet. They are usually air-conditioned, and though some may have seen better days, they usually get you to your destination without mishap. In peninsular Malaysia they are metered and reasonably priced, but make sure the driver turns the meter on; tourists are easy prey to taxi drivers who try to charge an inflated rate. Even so rates are generally very reasonable for Western visitors. In Sarawak and Sabah taxis are usually not metered and are more expensive; you have to bargain and agree upon the fare in advance. You are well advised to take a map and a pen and paper with you with your destination clearly indicated. Although you can usually make yourself understood you do on occasion get very blank stares and end up in totally the wrong place.

Charter Taxis

The long-distance charter taxis are a wonderful Malaysian institution. They are usually found at stands near bus stations or in other prominent parts of town. The driver waits until he gets four passengers; rates are very reasonable. If you are not in a party of four and you don't want to wait for a full load, you have to pick up the remaining fares; you can also travel in relative comfort. The drivers, however, can be adventurous and like to travel at high speed.

If you want to sightsee, in or out of town, you can negotiate a deal with a taxi driver for some hours. Some drivers are good tour guides, and will give you interesting information; others just want your money. But like taxi drivers the world over Malaysian drivers usually want to talk with you, and you can pick up all kinds of useful tips about the local scene and entertainment.

Improvements in the road system have made journeys much safer. Nevertheless, you have to note that road accidents are not rare in Malaysia, though the police are managing to curb some of the worst excesses of the Malaysian driver and are trying to enforce the speed limits (see pp.131–2).

BUSES

Buses are really good value, and ubiquitous. You can take long-distance air-conditioned express buses. There are usually conveniently located bus stations in towns and cities. Puduraya bus station in Kuala Lumpur is an exciting, manic place if you want to observe the colorful flotsam and jetsam of travelers spilling off vehicles and trying to board buses already overloaded with luggage and shopping. Traveling in Malaysia is also a social occasion. Malaysian friendliness means that you can always engage someone in conversation whether on a bus (which is the best transportation medium for engaging with local people), chartered taxi, or train. Rarely are you able to sit quietly when a local person sits next to you; they will want to find out about you, what you are doing, and whether you are enjoying your stay in Malaysia.

Town buses are fun and very cheap; you should experience them, though they can be noisy, crowded, and sometimes uncomfortable. But it is all part of the cross-cultural adventure. In Kuala Lumpur and some of the other main urban centers the minibuses are convenient, numerous, and frequent, but because they are smaller and more maneuverable than ordinary buses, drivers often have their own interpretation of where bus stops are located. This can work to your advantage, or not!

CARS AND RENTALS

If you want to be independent and drive yourself, there are many car rental agencies in Malaysia, from the internationally recognized, like Avis and Hertz, to the local. Expatriates and foreign visitors need a valid driver's license from their own country. A valid national or international license will allow you to drive in Malaysia for three months before you need to apply for a local license. To drive a car you must be over eighteen years of age, and of sound mind and body.

For car rental there are usually special three-day and weekend rates, and you should take out the appropriate additional insurance. Malaysians drive on the left, so it's slightly easier for the British and Irish than for visitors from North America. If you are driving in the Kuala Lumpur rush hours (and it is hours), sometimes you wonder whether there is any advantage in being accustomed to driving on the left, if you manage to move at all. Traffic jams in Kuala Lumpur are legendary. Lane discipline is not something that comes naturally and easily to the Kuala Lumpur driver, though once you get used to driving in the capital city there does seem to be some logic to it all. Also do not assume that people use their rearview mirrors, or that they signal where they are going, or that they will always pass on your right-hand side, or that they will park in designated parking spaces. Outside Kuala Lumpur everything else is smooth sailing. Drivers and passengers must wear seat belts, which does give you a higher level of reassurance and confidence.

Speed limits are 70 mph (110 kmph) on expressways, though in certain areas, for example on dangerous bends, it is reduced to 50–55 mph (80–90 kmph). On federal and state roads it is usually 55 mph (90 kmph) or again where necessary it is reduced to 50 mph (80 kmph). In towns the limit is 40mph (60 kmph) and for road safety purposes near schools or where there is heavy traffic for example it is reduced to 20 mph

(35 kmph). If you are in Malaysia at the time of a major festival you might find that speed limits are reduced. Fines for speeding are from 80 to 300 Malaysian dollars, depending on how much you have exceeded the limit.

If you are going to explore off the beaten path, especially in the wilds of Sarawak and Sabah, a four-wheel drive vehicle is essential. On the peninsula there is a good road network, with the tolled superhighway or expressway running from the Thai border via Kuala Lumpur to Singapore. But go with lots of cash—the tolls can add up. Near major urban and industrial centers roads are very busy and often clogged with slow-moving vehicles.

RAILWAYS

There is something rather romantic about traveling by rail in Malaysia on a railway system that was built during the late colonial period. The network is operated by the national railway company, Keretapi Tanah Melayu Berhad (KTMB), and the main line runs all the way from Singapore to Kuala Lumpur and to Butterworth (Penang), and then to the Thai border, with a number of branch lines. The station buildings and hotels in the main cities are listed buildings of great architectural interest.

There are three services: express with air-conditioning, and usually first- and second-class; limited express, which is somewhat slower, with some air-conditioning, but with third-class available as well; and the stop-anywhere, non-air-conditioned local trains (if you have a few days to spare and want to see the countryside). There is also a short stretch of railway in Sabah, which runs from Kota Kinabalu to Beaufort and Tenom; the western end of the journey runs through the spectacular scenery of the Crocker Range.

Currently the stretch of line between Kuala Lumpur and Ipoh is being upgraded, double-tracked, and electrified, partly to develop tourist business. It is due for completion in 2008, and will enable tourists to get to the northern part of the peninsula and Penang more quickly, and also open up the hidden delights of Ipoh, the "city built on tin," and a sadly neglected place on the tourist circuit that is well worth a visit.

Kuala Lumpur also has its own Light Rail Transit (LRT) system, sometimes referred to as "mass rapid transit" or "light rapid transit." The network is run by several private companies, including RapidKL, which runs the Ampang and Kelana Jaya lines, KL Monorail, and KTM Komuter. There is also the Express Rail Link (ERL), which runs a nonstop express (reaching a maximum speed of about 100 mph (160 kmph), as well as a commuter service on the 35-mile (57-km) track between KL International Airport and KL Sentral.

KL Sentral is the major hub for the LRT system. Airline passengers can also check in their luggage at KL Sentral before boarding the express train for KLIA. The first services were opened in 1996 and they proved a hit with visitors to the Commonwealth Games in 1998.

"Stuff Happens"

Once I took the train with my wife from Singapore to Kuala Lumpur to enjoy a rather different experience. We were delayed for six hours outside Johor Bahru because heavy rains had caused a landslide and blocked the track. Far from viewing scenery and landscapes, we spent most of the journey in the dark. We decamped to the restaurant car with four friendly and somewhat tipsy Sikh gentlemen who proceeded to recount their version of Malaysian history, and arrived in Kuala Lumpur just before midnight rather than early evening, worse for wear.

Traveling on the LRT is fun; some services run fully automated trains without drivers, others have a driver; some lines are raised above street level and give wonderful views of the cityscape. The LRT is easy to use; the route map is relatively simple and well set out. It covers all the main tourist destinations in and around the capital, and it's efficient and cheap. You can get out as far as the more distant suburbs of Rawang, Seremban, and Port Klang. You rarely have to wait longer than ten minutes for a train; during peak hours they run much more frequently, and a little less frequently on Sundays. You can purchase a day pass as well as integrated rail and bus passes, but a single LRT journey will only cost you between 70 cents and 2.90 Malaysian dollars.

BOATS

In Malaysian Borneo, aside from road and air travel, you may well find yourself on a boat. Given that the road system is still not extensive, there continues to be heavy reliance on river transport, especially if you are traveling into the interior. On the major rivers there are regular express-boat services with relatively low fares and on-boat video and musical entertainment. It is a good way to catch glimpses of jungle scenery and local longhouse and village communities while being blasted by popular music (Chinese and anything else) and scenes of Arnold Schwarzenegger exterminating all before him.

AIR TRAVEL

If you want to get from one place to another fast, and take in the major sights and resorts, then it has to be air travel, probably on the domestic carrier Malaysian Airlines. It serves all major towns and cities and, using small planes, many out-of-the-way places as well. There are regular shuttle services between Singapore and Kuala Lumpur, operated by both Malaysian Airlines and Singapore Airlines. There are also some very attractive deals to be had with Malaysian Airlines on the Discover Malaysia Pass, provided you have used the airline to enter the country, and there are other discounted tickets, for example for evening

travel. The airline is generally efficient, but do ensure that your booking is confirmed (overbooking is a problem, especially at holiday times). Other airlines serve various destinations in Malaysia outside the capital, including Penang, Kuching, and Kota Kinabalu.

HEALTH

You need to take a few simple precautions before traveling to Malaysia, especially if you are a first-time visitor. Medical insurance is essential, and you should seek advice from your own medical practitioner about the necessary inoculations and equip yourself with sufficient supplies of any other medication that you might need to take with you.

Vaccinations are not legally required for entry into Malaysia, but for those over one year of age and who have visited a country within the previous six days where there is yellow fever, a certificate of vaccination has to be presented.

There is a good range of state and private hospitals and clinics in the towns and cities of Malaysia, and numerous well-stocked pharmacies and chemists, but not necessarily in smaller settlements and out-of-the-way places.

The major inoculations advised for Malaysia are typhoid, tetanus, and hepatitis A. You may also need to seek advice about diphtheria, rabies, and hepatitis B. Dengue fever, malaria, and Japanese encephalitis are also present. If you are confining your visit to urban areas then you might not need to take a primary prophylactic against malaria, but if you are recommended to take antimalarial drugs you must start the course at least a week before departure and continue for at least four weeks after your return. You may find that the particular prescription will vary depending on precisely where you are intending to go; there are different strains of the parasite with different resistances. You should also purchase appropriate insect repellents, but it's best to get the recommended brand when you arrive.

Take care with drinking water (and ice) and make sure it is boiled or filtered and sterilized. Bottled mineral water is on sale everywhere. The Malay for water is *air* (pronounced "ah-yer").

Try to ensure, though it's sometimes difficult to do so, that meat and fish have been well cooked. Diarrhea isn't inevitable, but it's likely. Often it is relatively mild and results from a change of diet and eating spicy food. If it does become more serious then medication is required, and ample supplies of water to avoid dehydration. If in doubt consult a doctor.

Avoid too much sun and cover up when you are out. Use sunscreens and take note if you are sweating profusely, as you normally do in the humid tropics. Keep up your salt intake and drink plenty of water. Rather than serious infections you are more likely to suffer from skin problems —sunburn, insect bites and stings, prickly heat, rashes, and fungal infections. A supply of ointments, creams, and antihistamine is advisable.

SAFETY

Malaysia is a relatively safe place to visit, but take advice from your hotel or other local people about where you might visit and where you shouldn't, especially at night in large cities and towns. Open-air and usually crowded markets as well as public transportation are favorite places for pickpockets and purse snatchers in places like Kuala Lumpur. Don't walk around with a wallet, purse, or other valuables in full view or in easily accessible pockets or places.

You should ensure that you have photocopies or duplicates of all your important documents. Keep your passport and other travel documents and any surplus cash, as well as expensive jewelry, in a safe place. Most good-class hotels have room safes for the storage of some valuables, or you can make use of a secure box at reception. You should also have a record of important telephone numbers for credit card and insurance companies. Just use your common sense.

Malaysia is a very politically stable country, though there are currently some border problems occasioned by Muslim separatists in southern Thailand and northeastern Sabah. Take advice or consult the appropriate diplomatic mission if you are planning to visit northern peninsular Malaysia or travel from there to Thailand, or if you are visiting Sabah. There have been some cases of hijacking of vehicles and kidnappings. In addition, some areas in northern and eastern Sabah have been settled by Muslim people from the southern Philippines, and they have been involved in separatist activities against the Philippine government. Again, take care if you are traveling there.

chapter eight

BUSINESS BRIEFING

THE SOCIAL CONTEXT

As we have seen, Malaysians emphasize the importance of the family, the principle of trust and respect between members of a family and a wider social group, the importance of respect and deference between senior or high-status people and junior or those of low status, and the need to reach and maintain consensus and harmonious relations for personal, social, and spiritual reasons. These values are also expressed in the world of business and commerce. Remember, too, that ethnic identity is also a vitally important principle of organization in Malaysia, and this must also be borne in mind when doing business in the country. The business visitor to Malaysia must be prepared to move deftly and carefully along these sometimes tortuous social and cultural pathways.

THE IMPORTANCE OF RELATIONSHIPS

Given the importance of collective action and a communal ethos, the foreign businessperson in Malaysia has to be prepared to invest time in getting to know potential business partners.

Malaysians want to get to know you as a person. They want to know something about your character, background, status, and likes and dislikes. Malaysians rarely do business with someone whom they do not take to personally. In a fast-moving business world, where there may well be an expectation of making a deal as swiftly and efficiently as possible, there may be a degree of impatience to get down to business right away, but it is not appropriate etiquette to do so without first engaging in some small talk. Nor, following negotiations, should you expect immediate acceptances and decisions. A Malaysian will usually want to think it over and consult others.

The social element of doing business demands a significant level of face-to-face contact. Of course, e-mail, phone, fax, video conference, and other forms of electronic interaction are essential, but so is face-to-face interaction. E-mail enables you to arrange appointments with potential business partners with a minimum of fuss. You should usually do this well in advance through your own office. When you are in Malaysia, make a telephone call to your host's secretary or assistant to confirm the meeting. You may be requested to meet in the office or business premises, or for lunch or dinner in a hotel or restaurant. Business, office hours, and daily routine are given in Chapter 5.

SOCIAL INTERACTION

Social meetings, dinners, golf, and sometimes an invitation to a person's home (if relations are developing well) are part of the process of building confidence in a business relationship. Business deals may well be given a kick-start at the golf club or restaurant. With Chinese hosts you might also be encouraged to display your singing prowess in a karaoke bar.

These social events provide opportunities to get to know the pecking order and status of potential business partners, who the significant decision makers are, and who are the subordinates. The person who you think is the boss might not be, though the order in which people enter a room or restaurant usually indicates seniority, in that the most senior person enters first. Detailed negotiations may also not be undertaken by the most senior executive or the owner but instead by someone younger, more fluent in English, who has been trained in a business school.

The more extended the time spent in building relationships, the more you will be able to observe and learn the appropriate etiquette of respect, deference, and proper conduct in subsequent discussions and negotiations. Initially Malaysians can be relatively formal until they get to know you, but they are unfailingly polite. Too much informality at a first meeting can sometimes be interpreted as disrespectful. Although Malaysians do have a flexible view of time, you should always be punctual at business meetings, and during the meeting try to avoid looking at your watch as if you have somewhere else to go. You need to allow plenty of time for a meeting, and don't expect that it will end at a fixed or prearranged point.

CARDS AND CREDENTIALS

We have already discussed, in Chapter 4, the etiquette of greetings and first encounters in Malaysia, and dress. An additional dimension is the business card. Cards are a crucial part of business transactions in Malaysia, and they are also exchanged quite liberally at social functions. Your contact will normally give you a card that contains information about his title and status. Be sure to have an ample supply yourself—there is a degree of awkwardness to being given a card and having nothing to give in return.

The card should be received with the right hand, with some support from the left, or taken with both hands and studied attentively and respectfully. It should not be taken casually or indifferently and immediately slipped into a pocket. You have the donor's person and status in your hands. After the meeting, try to remember the face of the person that goes with the card for future reference, and during a meeting, if you are seated around a table, it may be useful to place the cards in front of you as a reminder of names, positions, and titles. It may be handy to have an indexed cardholder in your briefcase to keep them in some sort of order.

Given that so much emphasis is placed on the personal dimension of business relationships, it is also important to check out the credentials of potential business partners and their companies. They will have done their homework on you.

INTRODUCTIONS AND MEETINGS

On your first formal visit to a company, there may well be speeches of welcome and compliments from your hosts. You may have to introduce yourself and your company, and make a presentation. If you are introducing a product, or hoping to develop a joint project, go armed with a good supply of whatever will be helpful in the way of documents, samples, plans, brochures, or catalogs, or send them in advance.

Once business is under way, be clear in your own objectives, but, of course, be prepared to compromise. The deal is not concluded until it is set down in writing in a contract and signed. Malaysians often like to have formal signing ceremonies with photographs, speeches, and the exchange of gifts. Chinese business partners might also want to wait for an auspicious day in their calendar. Contracts are important, but Malaysians tend to seek personal trust and loyalty on a longer-term basis as well, and in this context Chinese partners might well ask for changes to the contract even after the contract has been signed.

GIFT GIVING

Malaysians love giving gifts, again as a sign of friendship or developing friendship, respect, gratitude, and as a memento to mark an event. However, tread very carefully in the whole area of gift giving, and seek advice from contacts and intermediaries about what is expected, reasonable, and appropriate. Bribery is officially condemned in Malaysia, which is clean in comparison with some other countries in the region. You can report cases of corruption to the Malaysian Anti-Corruption Agency, but you should be very sure of your evidence and before taking any drastic action talk it over with local and trusted colleagues and friends or with your diplomatic representatives. Of course, your prospective business partners will expect some good-quality entertainment and refreshment in return for their hospitality to you, and they will obviously want to treat you well. However, the distinction between gifts, donations, bribes, perks, commissions, and spin-offs can sometimes be difficult to determine.

PERSONAL BUSINESS

This issue is also complicated by the social dimension of relationships. Do not be surprised that Malaysian business operations are frequently based on close personal, family, ethnic, and patronage ties. Prominent Malay ex-civil servants and former politicians, as well as members of the royalty and nobility, are often closely interconnected in the higher levels of management and ownership of large state and various private sector companies. This principle operates in the private sector too, where Chinese interests based on family, clan, and dialect group help to determine employment, membership, and position. Influential Chinese and Malay businesspeople also sit together as boards of directors, and it is probably true to say that Malaysian business is dominated by a relatively small and closely connected and interrelated power elite. It is best to be circumspect when talking about the affairs of another company to your prospective business partners; they may also own or control it!

Likewise, don't be surprised if several people in a particular company or office are related. Though we in the West might think that people should be employed only on the basis of qualifications, merit, and skills, in Malaysia the obligations to kin and friends may well tip the balance, though these other factors are still important.

THE MALAYS AND BUSINESS

Given the dominant position of Malays in government and administration, though they are also increasingly seen in business, the foreign visitor chasing a public-sector contract or dealing with the authorities will usually have to enter discussions and negotiations with senior Malay bureaucrats. With civil servants such concerns as the national interest might outweigh those to do with pure profit, and political considerations might figure more prominently than commercial ones. Be mindful of the need to observe procedure and take the correct procedural steps. Be careful not to offend.

In private-sector negotiations one might also meet with Malay businesspeople as more and more Malays have been encouraged by government policy to take up commercial and industrial careers. Some have also gone into partnership with Chinese entrepreneurs, or Chinese companies have seen advantages in appointing prominent Malays to senior management positions and to their board of directors.

THE CHINESE AND BUSINESS

Nevertheless, the private sector, and especially retailing, trade, finance and construction, and small- and medium-sized companies, are still largely a Chinese preserve, and to a lesser extent Indian, where the profit motive is usually center stage, and the ethos is based much more on pragmatism and a flexible attitude toward market opportunities.

The foreign businessperson might also be faced with Chinese in business who come across as rather more aggressive and shrewd, although these characteristics are still often tempered by the Asian values of politeness, family, community, loyalty, hierarchy, and respect. Traditional Chinese social organization is based on the extended family focused on the male line and this is expressed in Chinese business life in terms of the importance of kinship, loyalty, and deference, and the relations between closely related circles of men.

There is a host of characteristics that have been used to explain the success of Chinese business: Confucian values of filial piety and loyalty, collectivism, clear lines of authority between seniors and juniors, the ethic of hard work, the effectiveness of personal networks or connections (*guanxi*), and the importance of trust (*sinyong*) and mutual understanding within the family firm and in intra-ethnic networks. These are elaborated on below. But it is important to note that cultural values are not fixed, stable, and unchanging, and nor do they necessarily directly determine behavior. They are often used selectively and according to situation, and they are used to justify a particular approach, position, or rationale. You may well find that the above value complex is expressed most frequently and positively by the older generation of Chinese businesspeople, often from a family-firm background. But the educated younger Chinese generation is not necessarily wedded to these values; behavior and attitudes will often vary according to age, education, experience, size and nature of the company, and so on.

You will find differences in management styles and business practices, especially outside the family-firm context and where government policy and experiences in an international business environment have served to give greater emphasis to doing business with non-Chinese and with reference to legal, institutional, and social class contexts, and not personal or ethnic ones. After all, Chinese family firms have broken up or been taken over in a competitive business environment and Chinese work with others beyond the Chinese community. Nevertheless, there seems to be a greater tendency among Chinese for the meshing of business and social affairs and for the importance of personal factors and networks. Remember the Chinese can and do operate in different modes, and can switch from Chinese values and practices to Western ones according to context.

BEWARE OF "TELLING IT LIKE IT IS"

The Westerner usually places a positive value on engaging openly in debate and in winning an argument by individual skill, fluency, and forcefulness. Emotions are deliberately put to one side. Malaysians recognize this pattern of behavior, but culturally they are much more concerned about the social context of interaction and with preserving harmony, balance, and consensus. Malaysians, and Malays especially, tend to be guided rather more by their emotions and inner feelings. They do not openly reveal these, but it is as well to be aware that this renders them personally more vulnerable in negotiation and argument. Elaborate codes of conduct are therefore ideal mechanisms for dealing with conflicts and tensions.

Emphasis is placed on courtesy, humility, tact, and deference. A very commonly used word in Malay is *malu* (shy, embarrassed, ashamed). *Malu* might be used to describe someone blushing over a personal remark made about them, or being shy in front of others, or to refer to the importance of being modest, courteous, and deferential. Juniors and inferiors in front of their seniors and superiors should show this sense of "shame."

There is a desire to reach agreement through consultation and compromise rather than by confrontation. It is important that no one should be offended, and no one publicly undermined. Losing face—being undermined or humiliated in public—causes shame and embarrassment. For this reason foreign business visitors should avoid, as far as possible, showing their emotions, particularly strong and negative emotions such as annoyance, irritation, anger, and impatience, and in a public forum "telling it like it is." They should never interrupt or talk over anyone.

The business visitor who might have occasion to reprimand someone should give some thought as

to how this should be done. To do so in public would be seen as as a personal insult, and might even be considered to augur bad luck. If an individual is at fault, he or she will feel bad about it. To confront him or her in front of others and expose wrongdoing, weakness, or shortcomings would be rude and thoughtless, and would moreover result in loss of esteem for you. In general, issuing commands and throwing your weight around are not appreciated.

An effective way of demonstrating concern or displeasure is through the use of an intermediary rather than face-to-face. This is an excellent rule of thumb if, as an expatriate, you are working in an office or business in Malaysia.

Nevertheless, it might still be difficult to determine if offense has been given and taken. It is usually through experience that one begins to pick up the subtle changes in manner, facial expression, and tone of voice that indicate that all is not well.

SMILES, NODS, AND SILENCES

The sparing of people's feelings and avoiding openly rejecting others and their opinions are important cultural requirements in Malaysia. It is better to be low-key and humble than self-assured and pompous. A very commonly used word in Malay is *ma'af* (sorry).

The Malaysian smile is a very versatile facial expression with a range of meanings. It can be used to avoid a direct confrontation. A smile and a nod accompanied by a "yes" might not be quite what they seem. To avoid open disagreement or offense, this might translate as simply "I hear you," or "I understand," but it might not indicate agreement. Sometimes it might cover incomprehension, when it would be impolite to say, "I don't understand."

A smile can also signify embarrassment, disagreement, or even annoyance. Malaysians do not usually like being put on the spot with a direct question, and there are various devices to cope with this, such as moving on to another topic, lapsing into chitchat, and, of course, the smile.

Be prepared for periods of silence. Malaysians are not uncomfortable if a meeting lapses into periodic silence. It is a time for reflection and weighing another's position. It can also take the heat out of a difficult situation and restore a balance and calmness to the proceedings.

WOMEN IN BUSINESS

As we have seen, Malaysian women are very evident in higher education. Although there are inequalities between men and women, women do occupy a relatively high status in society. They are also active in small and domestic businesses and have the reputation of being good with money and sound financial managers. They are found increasingly in business and the professions, though still mainly at the lower- and middle-management positions, and some are prominent in political life. Senior secretarial staff and personal assistants are frequently women, who therefore play a prominent role as office and business intermediaries. Muslim Malay women at work may well cover their heads, though not their faces, and wear the full-length skirt with a loose, long-sleeved blouse that extends to mid-thigh (*baju kurung*). Some may wear Western dress in the office. Western male visitors should observe the necessary Muslim etiquette and protocol and avoid being too familiar or informal in their behavior with women in the office.

Foreign businesswomen visiting Malaysia usually experience no problems in the business environment there and should not feel ill at ease because of their gender. They are treated with respect and politeness provided that they, in turn, observe the appropriate behavior and dress codes.

chapter nine

COMMUNICATING

THE NATIONAL LANGUAGE

Bahasa Malaysia, "the Malaysian Language," is the official language, and is a standardized form of the Malay language, or Bahasa Melayu. With some variations it is also the official language of neighboring Indonesia, Brunei, and Singapore. It is a major language within the broader and very diverse family of Austronesian, which is found as far afield as Madagascar, southern Vietnam, the Philippines, and through the Pacific, including New Zealand and Hawaii, to Easter Island.

The earliest form of Malay is thought to have originated in western Borneo (though there is still academic debate about this), but it certainly developed in Sumatra and was later disseminated as a language of trade. It was liberally sprinkled with elements of Arabic, Indian, Chinese, Portuguese, Dutch, and English.

Malaysians, with their different backgrounds, will have knowledge of Malay to varying degrees and levels of proficiency, though there are also considerable variations in dialects, and these may diverge from the national language. A widely used, everyday form of Malay, or pidgin Malay, which can be heard in the streets and markets, used by Chinese shopkeepers for example, is appropriately called "bazaar Malay" (*Melayu pasar*).

Malay has a traditional script called Jawi, which is based on Arabic, but the written language has long been Romanized. Therefore, you can read it, even if you do not understand it. It's a good idea to buy an up-to-date English–Malay pocket guide, available in airport bookstores and local bookshops. The language, like all languages, is constantly evolving—so buy the newest edition.

To engage with local people and learn something of the local culture, it is worth the effort to learn some words of Malay. Some basic vocabulary and everyday sentences are relatively easy; but you may find that local people will still respond to you in English!

Tips on Spelling and Pronunciation
Some "problem" consonants are pronounced as follows:
c as in *cat* (paint) is "ch," as in "chat"
g as in *garam* (salt) is hard, as in "good"
h in *hitam* (black) is soft, but usually not pronounced
kh as in *khusus* (special) is a hard "k"
ng in *dengar* (to hear) is soft, as in "song"
ngg in *mangga* (mango) is hard, as in "tango"
sy in *syarikat* (a company) is pronounced "sh," as in "shutter"
r as in *baru* (new) is trilled or rolled

Malay, like English, has five vowels: *a e i o u; i o u* are long; *a* is short, and *e* can be unaccented, like the "u" in English "put," or stressed, as in French. There are two diphthongs: *au* (as in "how"), and *ai* (as in "die").

MALAYSIAN ENGLISH

English is widely used in Malaysia, in the media, and in higher education, and is the preferred language of business and tourism. You will have no difficulty finding local people who will speak to you in English. However, you should take the trouble to speak clearly, at a moderate pace, using complete sentences. Conversely, an old Cantonese taxi driver with few teeth asking you rapidly in English, or more accurately Malaysian-Chinese English, where you wish to go in Kuala Lumpur can also be something of a challenge.

The Malaysians have developed their own English style, and Chinese Malaysians in particular have adapted and abbreviated English for their own purposes. The word "can" is especially versatile. As in the English colloquialism "Can do," it means "Yes," "I can do it," or "It's possible," while "Also can" is a little less positive. "Cannot" is the obvious negative response. "How can" is even more emphatically negative, and if someone asks for something unreasonably then a likely negative response is "Where got." "Can ah?" is asking if something can be done, or if it's possible or all right. Without the interrogation, "Can ah" gives permission.

There is also the very common use of the word "*lah*" to round off a sentence. It may or may not be used for emphasis. "Last time" is a general referent for the past or past tense and "Next time" is used for the future.

Malaysians also mix English and Malay. Rather than use the English word "eat," Malaysians prefer their own word, *makan;* so might say, "Shall we *makan?*" or "Let's go for *makan*" or, if suggesting a drink, "Let's *minum.*" The importance of having a bath or shower in the tropics also ensures that the Malay word *mandi* is used frequently. Before eating it might be suggested that you might "*Mandi* first" (*mandi dulu*).

Something Familiar?

If you are an English-speaker you will notice some Malay words, such as *ambulans, aspirin, bank, doktor,* and *telefon*, that are reassuringly close to their English equivalents. Try these: *bas, beg, bir, farmasi, filem, kaunter, minit, polis, pos, stem, stesyen, teksi.* The translations are jumbled in the following list: police, minute, counter, bus, stamp, beer, bag/baggage, film, pharmacy, taxi, post, and station. Good luck!

Some Basic Vocabulary and Expressions

It is certainly worth learning a few stock phrases of Bahasa Malaysia. Malaysians will appreciate your efforts and it is a good way of establishing rapport and interacting with local people in a more meaningful and intimate way.

Selamat pagi, selamat tengahari, selamat petang, and selamat malam are "good morning," "good day (midday)," "good afternoon," and "good evening" (*selamat* literally means "peaceful"). These are relatively formal greetings. Another set of "peaceful" greetings is *selamat datang* (welcome), *selamat tinggal* (good-bye, said by the person leaving), *selamat jalan* (good-bye, bon voyage, said by the one staying behind), and *sampai jumpa lagi* (until we meet again).

A more informal greeting is to ask, *Apa khabar?* (How are you?, or, literally, What news?). A simple response, (*khabar*) *baik* (fine), will suffice. Another useful word is *bagus* (good). You might then want to ask someone's name: *Apa nama anda/kamu?* (What is your name?), and say *Nama saya—* (My name is —).

Other useful words for an initial exchange include directions: *darimana?* (from where?), *kemana?* (where to?), *dimana?* (where?). *Dari, ke,* and *di* translate as "from," "to," and "in" or "at;" *kanan* "right," and *kiri* , "left." It might be useful to ask where someone originates from: *Berasal darimana?* The response is *Saya berasal dari—.* Malaysian preoccupations with social and family background might also prompt queries about marital status: *Encik sudah berkawin?* (Are you married?); *Berapa orang anak tuan/puan?* (Do you have children?).

Finally, other common and useful words in everyday conversation are: *ya* (yes), *tidak* (no), *belum* (not yet), *ma'af* (sorry, excuse me), *minta ma'af* (to beg pardon), *hari ini* (today, literally, this day), *besok* (tomorrow), *semalam, kelmarin* (yesterday), *makan* (eat), *minum* (drink), *saya mau* (I would like), *saya tidak mau* (I do not want), *beli* (buy), *saya tidak mengerti* (I do not understand), *terima kasih* (thank you), *terima kasih banyak* (thank you very much), *sila* or *mari* (please [go ahead]), *tolong* (please [request for help]), *minta* (please [request for something]), *laki-laki* (male), *lelaki* (man), *perempuan* (woman), *orang* (person).

The numerals from one to ten are: *satu, dua, tiga, empat, lima, enam, tujuh, lapan, sembilan, sepuluh.* One hundred is *seratus,* and one thousand *seribu.*

It's also fun to learn some key words from menus so that you can order food in restaurants. The words for basic ingredients and drinks are very easy to learn, not least the Malay for rice, *nasi,* and fried rice, *nasi goreng,* and the Chinese word for noodles, *mee,* which Malays also use. The words for tea and coffee are *the* and *kopi,* but the variety of ways in which Malaysians have adapted these drinks have given rise to many other words, which you will soon pick up.

This brief excursion into Malay should get you on your way, at least for the short-term tourist and business visitor.

OTHER LANGUAGES

In Malaysia's multiethnic and multicultural society many other languages are also commonly used: Mandarin, and a variety of southern Chinese dialects including Cantonese and Hokkien, several Indian languages, particularly Tamil, and the numerous native languages of Borneo.

For the really ambitious, particularly those in business, it might be worth learning Mandarin, and, as the strength of mainland China's economy grows, this becomes an increasingly attractive proposition. But be warned, it is a very difficult language to master. If you want to give it a try, be prepared to devote long hours to intensive study.

BODY LANGUAGE

As we have already seen, in Chapters 4 and 8, there is a developed etiquette and use of gestures, facial expression, and postures in Malaysia. Here are some of the more important dos and don'ts.

- Don't give or receive things with your left hand.
- Don't point or beckon with your index finger.
- Don't point your foot at anyone.
- Don't show the soles of your shoes or feet.
- Don't grasp anyone's hand in a firm handshake.
- Don't shake a woman's hand unless she offers it.
- Don't touch, embrace, or kiss someone of the opposite sex in public.
- Don't touch anyone's head or hair.
- Don't stand with your hands on your hips.
- Don't speak loudly or aggressively.

- Don't publicly reprimand or embarrass anyone.
- Don't display your feelings openly.

- Do be tactful and polite.
- Do show respect to your seniors.
- Do address people using their correct title.
- Do remove your shoes when entering someone's house or a mosque.
- Do dress modestly and conservatively.
- Do be patient and calm during meetings and social encounters.
- Do speak clearly, gently, and in a measured way.
- Do show interest in local cultures, cuisine, and language.

MEANS OF COMMUNICATION

There is a wide range of media services and access to news and information. However, the Malaysian government keeps a close eye on public criticism and political opposition, and the level of public debate is lower than in the West. There is strict censorship of publications, films, programs, and performances deemed to be counter to Malaysian, particularly Muslim, values of decency. Several Western popular musicians have been banned. There is also control over government-owned media reporting on sensitive issues. However, there are privately owned and operated media companies, and there are some Malaysian-based Internet sources critical of the government that are tolerated.

Telephone, E-mail, and Mail Services

The provision of fixed-line telephones, largely monopolized by Telekom Malaysia (TM), in which the government holds a large stake, covers only about a quarter of the population. The national and international service in towns and cities and from business premises and hotels is usually very good. However, there has been a boom in cell phone use, and there are estimated to be 20 million cell phones in Malaysia. The main providers of cell phone services are TM's Celcom, as well as Maxis, DiGi, and U Mobile.

There has also been a rapid increase in Internet and e-mail use, with 13.5 million users (about half the population), though broadband is not widely used. For the Internet TM Net is dominant, along with Jaring. Cyber cafés are especially popular among the young.

The postal service run by Pos Malaysia and referred to as "snail mail" is quite reliable; it has a more expensive express service (*poslaju*) as well.

The Media

The Press

The most popular English-language newspaper, established in 1845, is the *New Straits Times*, which also has a Sunday edition and an online version. Other English-language papers are *The Star*, *The Sun*, *Business Times*, and *The Sarawak Tribune*. There are numerous Malay and Chinese-language dailies.

There is considerable choice of Internet news services; the government operates its own Bernama News Agency that gives the official government line; other news providers are Reuters Malaysia and Focus on Malaysia. A service that provides a more critical and independent view of Malaysian affairs, and which is very widely used, is the Malaysia-based Malaysiakini.com, as well as the news blog Malaysia Today.

Television and Radio
Malaysia has a relatively wide choice of TV and radio programs. There are six free-to-air TV channels, among them those provided by the government-owned Radio Televisyen Malaysia (RTM), which operates TV1, TV2, and a digital channel; it also runs eight national, sixteen state, and seven district radio stations; there are also private radio stations.

TV1 has educational, local information, news, and entertainment programs in Malay and English. TV2 provides entertainment programs and films in Malay, English, Chinese, Tamil, and Hindi, and even Korean, Thai, and Spanish. The most popular channel is TV3, mainly providing entertainment in Malay and English, and operated by the independent Media Prima Berhad, which also runs ntv7, TV8, and TV9. There is an in-house hotel entertainment service, Vision Four. Pay-per-view satellite networks, mainly in English, are operated by the private companies Astro, Cosmos Discovery, and Fine TV.

CONCLUSION

Malaysia is a culturally diverse and endlessly fascinating country. Excursions into the countryside, the national parks, and the upriver regions are a must, and Malaysian cuisine provides the best that Asia has to offer. The visitor will feel part of a vibrant, dynamic, fast developing, modernizing society, and will at the same time find much that is intriguingly different. For city lovers, its cultural, ethnic, and heritage resources are a major attraction; for outdoor types ecotourism is another fast expanding sector; and for those in business the opportunities are exciting.

This brief overview of the cultural context behind the cautionary dos and don'ts is designed to help you navigate the unfamiliar. Beyond the great cultural diversity there are shared values and principles that underlie Malaysian behavior and etiquette: the emphasis on status, hierarchy, respect, deference, politeness, modesty, harmony, calmness, consensus, face, and spirituality,

balanced by a relatively relaxed and give-and-take attitude to life. This means that the foreign visitor needs to show understanding and sensitivity, but should not get too anxious if things go wrong. Malaysians will welcome you and accept your shortcomings if you show interest, respect, and a willingness to learn and to engage with them and their country.

Further Reading

History and Politics
There is an enormous literature on Malaysia in English, though it often focuses on either the Malayan Peninsula or British Malaya, and then separately on Sarawak and British North Borneo, or Sabah. Some of the best general histories are:

Andaya, Barbara Watson and Leonard Y. Andaya. *A History of Malaysia*, Basingstoke: Palgrave, 2001 (second edition).

Crouch, Harold. *Government and Society in Malaysia*. Ithaca, New York: Cornell University Press, 1996.

Gullick, J. M. *Malaysia and its Neighbors*. London: Routledge and Kegan Paul, 1967.

Gullick, J. M. *Old Kuala Lumpur*. New York: Oxford University Press, 1994.

Hooker, Virginia Matheson. *A Short History of Malaysia: Looking East and West*, St Leonards, NSW: Allen and Unwin, 2003.

Turnbull, C. Mary. *A Short History of Malaysia, Singapore and Brunei*. Singapore: Graham Brash, 1980.

Literature
For a more literary approach to Malaysian perspectives and history:
Hooker, Virginia Matheson. *Writing a New Society: Social Change through the Novel in Malay*. Honolulu: University of Hawai'i Press, 2000.

Popular Reading and Travel
There are also very useful paperback series published by Oxford University Press in Singapore and Kuala Lumpur in the 1980s and 1990s (Oxford in Asia Paperbacks), many of which are still in print. They comprise reprints of classic travel and other writings on Malaysia and the region as well as anthologies of travel writing for light reading. The series include:

Gullick, J. M. *Adventures and Encounters: Europeans in South-East Asia*, and *They Came to Malaya*.

King, Victor T. *The Best of Borneo Travel* and *Moving Pictures. More Borneo Travel*.

Knappert, Jan (ed. Graham Saunders). *Mythology and Folklore in South-East Asia*.

Saunders, Graham. *Tropical Interludes: European Life and Society in South-East Asia*.

Waterson, Roxana. *The Architecture of South-East Asia Through Travellers' Eyes*.

Two edited books, useful but which unfortunately impose a rather gendered view on exploration (a male domain) and travel (a female domain) are:

Gullick, J.M. *Adventurous Women in South-East Asia: Six Lives*.

King, Victor T. *Explorers of South-East Asia: Six Lives*.

Copyright © 2008 Kuperard
Fourth printing 2014

All rights reserved. No part of this publication may be reprinted or reproduced, stored in a retrieval system, or transmitted in any form or by any means without prior permission in writing from the publishers.

Culture Smart!® is a registered trademark of Bravo Ltd.

Index